Interview

How To Prepare For Your Next Job Interview And Answer Questions Smartly With Confident Body Language & Start The Career Of Your Dreams

(How To Have A Winning Approach To Interview)

Eliseo Neal

Published by Rob Miles

Eliseo Neal

All Rights Reserved

Interview: How To Prepare For Your Next Job Interview And Answer Questions Smartly With Confident Body Language & Start The Career Of Your Dreams (How To Have A Winning Approach To Interview)

ISBN 978-1-989990-73-5

All rights reserved. No part of this guide may be reproduced in any form without permission in writing from the publisher except in the case of brief quotations embodied in critical articles or reviews.

Legal & Disclaimer

The information contained in this book is not designed to replace or take the place of any form of medicine or professional medical advice. The information in this book has been provided for educational and entertainment purposes only.

The information contained in this book has been compiled from sources deemed reliable, and it is accurate to the best of the Author's knowledge; however, the Author cannot guarantee its accuracy and validity and cannot be held liable for any errors or omissions. Changes are periodically made to this book. You must consult your doctor or get professional medical advice before using any of the suggested remedies, techniques, or information in this book.

Upon using the information contained in this book, you agree to hold harmless the Author from and against any damages, costs, and expenses, including any legal fees potentially resulting from the application of any of the information provided by this guide. This disclaimer applies to any damages or injury caused by the use and application, whether directly or indirectly, of any advice or information presented, whether for breach of contract, tort, negligence, personal injury, criminal intent, or under any other cause of action.

You agree to accept all risks of using the information presented inside this book. You need to consult a professional medical practitioner in order to ensure you are both able and healthy enough to participate in this program.

Table of Contents

INTRODUCTION 1

CHAPTER 1: PREPARING PHYSICALLY AND PSYCHOLOGICALLY FOR THE INTERVIEW 4

CHAPTER 2: GEARING UP: SUIT UP, ARM YOURSELF AND DO NOT BE CAUGHT OFF GUARD 12

CHAPTER 3: PREPARING TO THE JOB INTERVIEW 17

CHAPTER 4: PROFESSIONAL ETIQUETTE AND THE ONSITE INTERVIEW 23

CHAPTER 5: USING BODY LANGUAGE 26

CHAPTER 6: COVER LETTER – YOUR GRAND ENTRANCE ... 37

CHAPTER 7: DO YOUR RESEARCH 42

CHAPTER 8: THE APPROPRIATE WAY TO APPEAR FOR AN INTERVIEW 56

CHAPTER 9: HOW TO CREATE COVER LETTERS THAT GET GREAT RESULTS 62

CHAPTER 10: DEALING WITH INTERVIEW QUESTIONS: POSSIBLE QUESTIONS TO EXPECT AND QUESTIONS TO ASK 70

CHAPTER 11: THE RIGHT LOOK 83

CHAPTER 12: CAPABILITIES & FACING CHALLENGES 93

CHAPTER 13: THE SWOT ANALYSIS 100

CHAPTER 14: THE PHONE INTERVIEW! 106

- CHAPTER 15: PUT FORTH CONFIDENCE IN THE INTERVIEW 117
- CHAPTER 16: HOW TO SEARCH FOR A JOB? 125
- CHAPTER 17: WHAT TO DO AFTER THE INTERVIEW 131
- CHAPTER 18: SELLING YOURSELF; AN ELEVATOR PITCH. 137
- CHAPTER 19: MAIN TYPES OF INTERVIEWS 141
- CHAPTER 20: POPULAR INTERVIEW QUESTIONS 158
- CHAPTER 21: 10 MUST PREPARED INTERVIEW QUESTIONS 175
- CHAPTER 22: TYPES OF INTERVIEW QUESTIONS 182
- CONCLUSION 192

Introduction

All Of My Part-Time Jobs As A Kid Growing Up Were With Businesses Run By Family Friends, Or Laboring Jobs That Simply Didn't Require An Interview Process. After Finishing University, I Suddenly Found Myself Out In The 'Real World', With No Interviewing Experience To Help Me To Get Through The Insanely Difficult And Stringent Processes Companies Put Me Through. Going For Interviews Was Hard! I Was Practically Falling At The First Hurdle In Each Interview Because I Didn't Know What I Needed To Take In, How To Prepare Beforehand And How To Act When I Was In The Interview. If I Went In Too Casual The Interviewers Would Tell Me That I Was Unprepared And Not Taking The Interview Seriously, While If I Tried To Prepare I Often Became Overwhelmed And Was A Nervous Wreck By The Time I Went In For The Actual Interview.

It Took Me A Lot Of Practice And Countless Interviews Before I Eventually Managed To Even Become Comfortable In An Interview Situation, But Thankfully I Learned More And More With Each One I Went Through. I Finally Discovered That Interviewing For A Job Isn't As Intimidating As It Once Seemed. I Found Out That If I Followed A Set Procedure In Preparation For The Interview, And Behaved In The Correct Way During It, I Could Nail Each And Every Interview I Went In To. Soon Enough Instead Of Being Desperate And Limited For Job Opportunities, I Had The Pick Of Any Job I Applied For Because My Interviewing Skills Were Better Than All Of The Other Candidates.

By Now I've Applied And Been Successful With Several Different Companies In Quite Different Roles. I Now Know Exactly What It Takes To Be Successful In Any Interview Situation, And I'm Positive That The Process I'm About To Outline Can Work For Anyone Applying For A Job In Any Field. While There Will Be Some Work Required On Your Behalf, If You Follow

This General Outline On How To Efficiently And Effectively Prepare For And Handle The Interviewing Process, You Will Give Yourself The Greatest Chance Of Success In Any Job Application.

I Wish You The Best Of Luck In Your Future Endeavors And Again Want To Thank You For Downloading This Book. I Trust And Believe That I Can Help You To Achieve Your Highest Potential.

Chapter 1: Preparing Physically And Psychologically For The Interview

Congratulations! You Were Patient (We Hope!) And Have Landed An Interview. The Next Step Is The Physical Appearance And Personal Interaction Element To Be Prepared For Your Interview. This Might Seem Like Common Sense, But It Is Very Crucial That The Interview Progresses Well And That The Interviewer Has An Excellent Opinion Of You For The Best Chance To Be Hired. There Are Likely Many Other Applicants And The Job Can Be Yours If You Can Get Past This Part With Flying Colors!

At This Stage We Shall Comprehensively Cover How To Prepare For An Interview, How To Dress Before An Interview (Grooming), Body Language, What To Avoid Before And During An Interview And How To Get The Best Out Of An Interview Session.

How To Prepare For An Interview/Pre-Interview Preparation

Your Main Objective The Moment You Get Interviewed By Any Hiring Team Should Always Be To Showcase Your Skills And Convince The Team Meant To Hire You. You Are Selling Yourself Through Your Professional Appearance, Demeanor And You Need To Command Confidence And Respect. Prove To The Hiring Team That You Have The Experience, Knowledge And Skills To Be Part Of Their Team And Contribute To The Growth Of The Organization. Tell Them That You Are More Than Willing To Go An Extra Mile To See The Company Grow And Make More Profits. Say Yes When They Ask About Working Overtime Or Possibly Relocating (If You Are Willing To). The More You Are Open To As It Relates Directly To The Job, The More You Will Be Favored When It Is Decision Time.

Pre- Interview Preparation

Do Your Research About The Organization Or Company Which Has Scheduled For Your Interview. This Is An Important Meeting So Prepare, Prepare, Prepare.

You Should Always Have The Right Background Information About The Company In Order To Have The Best Potential Of Landing The Job.

☐ Research On The Plans Already Underway To Steer Growth, Stability And Development Of The Organization. If There Are No Plans, Prepare To Tell The Hiring Team That You Are Willing To Contribute To Their Growth And Back This Up With Statistical Proof Mirroring A Fact You Stated In Either Your Cover Letter Or Resume. For Example, "…From 2012 To 2014, I Helped Raise Store Sales Growth By 10% By Increased Use Of Customer Receipt Surveys." Be Prepared To Speak In Depth About The Process.

☐If The Company Has A Monthly Newsletter, Read It Cover-To-Cover To Be In-The-Know About Upcoming Events Or Exciting News That Could Potentially Come Up In The Conversation Between The Interviewer And Yourself.

☐ Seek Out Who The Most Substantial Clients Or Contracts Are With, Their Marketing Strategy,

Strengths/Weaknesses And Their Strategic Plan. A Good Place For This Is The Company Website And Any Related Websites. Know Their Affiliates Or Any Associated Companies. Study The "About Us" Page In Detail. Also Read Reviews, Good And Bad, To Help Determine The Strengths And Weaknesses Of The Company In Question.

☐ Research Any New Product Or Service Offerings, Potential Company Risks, And Whether Revenues Are Growing Or Have A Stable Pattern.

☐ Review Their Vision, Mission And Objectives.

☐ Study Their "Social Responsibility" Initiatives. Be Sure To Mention If You Have Any Volunteer Experience With Any Charities Or Organizations That They Assist Or Donate To. On The Other Hand, If They Are Not Involved With Any Charity Work, Volunteering Or Community Involvement, Be Leery Of The Company.

☐ Research The Company On Social Media And Read The News Feed.

☐ Do A Google Search On The Company And Read Any Relevant News Or Happenings.

One Last Important Note - Be Sure To Examine The Hierarchy Of The Organization And Find Out Where The Job Position Fits. Learn Who You Will Report To And Who Will Report To You. If This Is Not Possible, Learn About The Infrastructure Of Similar Organizations So That You Will Be Somewhat Knowledgeable About The Internal Hierarchy.

Get Insider Information About Your Interviewer If Possible

Ask About The Person Who Will Be Interviewing You. Whether It Is Hr Or The Manager, It Is Helpful To Know The Person Who Will Conduct The Interview So That You Can Come Up With A Strategy To Meet Their Expectations. This Is Not Possible In Some Circumstances And That Is Okay. If You Cannot Get Inside Information As To The Interviewer, By Following The Steps Provided In This Book,

The Interviewer Should Be Impressed With You By The Time Your Interview Is Over.

How To Dress To Impress For Your Job Interview

Dress Yourself In A Professional Manner

If The Atmosphere Is A Special Type Such As A Doctor's Office Or Veterinary Office Where The Majority Of Employees Are Wearing Scrubs Or Casual Clothing, Then It May Be Acceptable To Dress Down A Bit, Such As Wearing A Blouse And Khaki Pants. When In Doubt, However, Professional Attire Such As A Suit Is The Standard. It Is Better To Be A Little Overdressed Then Underdressed And Possibly Lose Out On The Position. For Men, The Standard Should Always Be A Suit And Tie.

Prepare The Night Before

Lay Out Your Clothes And Accessories The Night Before. While Going On An Interview Is Stressful Enough, Having Your Clothes Ready For You Will Be One Less Thing To Feel Stressed Out About On The Big Day. If Your Clothes Are Laid Out, Ironed And Ready To Be Put On, It May

Help You Feel Less Anxious And More Organized So You Can Focus On The Interview Itself.

Your Potential Employer Is More Likely To Tell The Kind Of A Person You Are By The First Impression You Make During An Interview. The Hiring Team Is Most Likely To Judge You By The Way You Dress And Your General Appearance.

Men

-Suit (Official Colors Such As Grey Or Navy)
-White Shirt (Long Sleeve)
-Belt (Color Should Match Your Shoes)
-Tie
-Avoid Jewelry Except For A Wedding Ring, If Applicable
-Trimmed Nails
-Portfolio Or Professional Carrying Case
-Dark Socks
-Shaven Or Short, Trimmed Facial Hair

Women

-Suit
-Dress Shoes Which May Include Pumps, Standard Heels (3" At The Most) Or Flats
-Professional Blouse That Matches With Your Suit

-Avoid Excessive Jewelry. Nothing Dangly. Small Earrings, Such As Small Hoops, Studs Or Pearls Are Acceptable.

-Portfolio Or Professional Carrying Case

-Neat, Trimmed Nails. A Subtle Painted Color Is Acceptable.

-Avoid Excessive Make-Up. Less Is More Here.

Men And Women

-Neat, Clean And Simple Hair Style. It Should Represent A Professional Appearance And Not Cover Your Eyes In Any Way.

-Absolutely No Piercings Except Those In Your Ears. This Goes For Any Position At Any Job. It's An Absolute Deal-Breaker For Any Job.

-Cover Any Tattoos In Obvious Places. There Is Special Cover-Up Make-Up That You Can Purchase In Most Pharmacies Or Department Stores That Can Cover Tattoos In Obvious Spots On Your Body.

Chapter 2: Gearing Up: Suit Up, Arm Yourself And Do Not Be Caught Off Guard

You Know The Saying That Goes "By Failing To Prepare, You Are Preparing To Fail"? Well, That Could Not Be Truer For A Job Interview. No Matter What Kind Of Interview You Will Be Going Through, It Pays To Be Very Prepared.

What You Should Expect

1. The Interviewer Is Not Always Going To Be Friendly

It Is The Interviewer's Job To See How Qualified You Are For The Job So You Can Expect To Get A Serious Tone Of Voice And Demeanor, Bordering On Intimidating (Or Scary!) When You Go On An Interview. The Interviewer Will Scrutinize You In Every Way Possible And This Person Is Trained To See Through Your Being, So To Speak. So No, You Cannot Lie About Your Qualifications Because They Will Most Likely Find Out. And No, That Smile Does Not Automatically Mean The Interviewer Is Impressed With You. It Could Be That You

Hair Looks Funny Or You Committed A Typographical Error Somewhere In Your Documents.

Expecting The Interviewer To Be Unfriendly And Intimidating May Be A Terrifying Thought But This Is A Fact Of Life. There Are More Badass Interviewers Out There Than Cutesy Ones So You Are Better Equipped If You Expect A Stern And Serious Interviewer. Besides, You Are Applying For A Job; You're Not Trying To Make Friends—Think Of The Interviewer As The Gatekeeper Who Will Not Let You Get Through Unless You Have The Right Stuff!

2. You Will Be Asked Tons Of Questions

This Is Sort Of A No-Brainer. It's An Interview; You Will Be Asked Questions About Yourself And Your Qualifications. Think Of It This Way, The More Questions You Are Asked, The More Interested They Are About You. We Will Tackle Questions More In A Different Chapter.

3. Other Applicants Are Also Going To Be Interviewed

Whether You Are Applying For A Small Company Or A Large Multi-National One, You Have To Know That You Are Probably Not The Only One They Have On The List Of Applicants. You Just Be One In A Line Of A Hundred Or So. Do Not Let The Simple Act Of Getting An Interview Schedule Go Up To Your Head, Do Not Stop Looking For Other Jobs And Do Not Leave You Existing Job Just Because You Are Getting An Interview Somewhere Else. It's Only Just An Interview; You Have Not Landed The Job Yet.

4. That The Interview Schedule Given To You Will Be Followed To The Time

The Schedule You Will Be Given Has An Exact Time And Location For A Reason – The People Involved In The Interview Have Other Things To Do Like Interview Others Or Manage Other People At The Workplace. So You Can Expect That The Time Slot Given To You Is Limited To That. Were You Not Given A Time Frame? Do Not Hesitate To Ask The Person Who Contacted You So You Can Be Sure.

5. You Have About One Minute (60 Seconds) To Answer Each Question

There Are No Hard And Fast Rules On How Long An Answer To An Interview Question Should Take. However, You Should Remember That Your Interview Time Is Limited And That The Most Brief And Concise Answer Will Suffice. Beating Around The Bush Will Just Make You Look Unsure And Unconfident, So Try To Limit Your Answer To About 60 Seconds. If The Interviewer Asks You To Explain Further, Then You Can Go Ahead And Add To Your Answer. Do Not Be A Drag; You Do Not Want The Interviewer To Fall Asleep While You Go On A Storytelling. Go Straight To The Point, That's The Best Thing To Do.

6. That The Interviewer Has Looked At Your Resume And Has Done Some Sort Of Background Check Beforehand

It Is Quite Common For Hiring Managers To Make Calls And Verify Your Information, And Look You Up On The Internet To Have A Fair Idea Of What Kind Of Person You Are. Expect That This Little Research That They Did Helped Them

Come Up With The Questions To Ask You. Also, Expect That Some Work-Related Issues May Surface, Especially If Your Last Employment Did Not End So Amicably. The Good News About Expecting These Though Is That You Can Prepare Answers And Not Look Stupid If Ever Some Harder Questions Come Up During Your Interview Proper.

Chapter 3: Preparing To The Job Interview

What To Bring With You?

Preparing Yourself With What You Have To Say Before, During, And After The Interview Isn't The Only Important Thing You Need To Look At; There Are Also Several Items You Need To Prepare When You Are Going For A Job Interview. In This Part, We Will Tell Some Of The Important Things You Need To For The Job Interview.

Multiple Copies Of Your Resume

You Already Know The Importance A Resume And How Important It Is To Put It Up The Right Way, However, You Have To Know That It's Always To Bring Multiple Copies Of It With You When Going For An Interview. So, Why Does It Matter If You Have Multiple Resumes Or Not? Well, You Will Never Know! What If There Is A Panel Of Interviewers In The Room? Giving Resume To Each Of Them Will Give Them An Impression That You Are Always Prepared. It's Also A Good Idea Because As You Might Find Another Opening Position

For Another Company Where You Can Submit Your Resume To.

A Notebook And A Pen

This Will Let You Take Notes Of Important Things The Interviewer Say During The Interview. You Could Also Write Down The Questions You Would Like To Ask The Interviewer When It's Your Time To Talk. When The Interview Ends, You Can Sit Down Somewhere And Write Down Your Impressions Of The Company, All The Questions They Asked You, The Good Things About The Interview, And The Ones You Can Improve. Discipline Might Be Necessary For Taking Notes, But Imagine How Ready You Will Feel If They Notify You For Another Interview? You Will Be Confident That You Will Ace The Next Interview.

Book And Snacks

So, Why These Items, You May Ask. Well, You May Need To Wait For Your Turn To Get Interviewed, So In Order To Keep You From Boredom Bring Something That Will Entertain You In The Form Of Reading

Material. You Also Don't Want To Have An Interview While You Are Hungry.

The Right Bag

It's Important That You Bring The Right Kind Of Bag With You When Going To A Job Interview. For Men, It's Suggested To Bring A Leather Briefcase, While For Women A Shoulder Bag Would Be Nice. Make Sure That The Bag Is Professional Looking And Is Able To Carry Everything You Need.

By Preparing These What Seem To Be Trivial You Will Boost Your Chances Of Getting Hired For The Job You Are Applying For.

Appropriate Clothing

When Going For A Job Interview, You're Probably Aware Of The Importance Of Wearing The Proper Clothing As It Will Make A Good Impression On You. It's Normal As The Most Important Thing For You Is To Impress Your Potential Employer And You Would Like To Send A Message That You're The Perfect Candidate For The Job. Here Are Some Tips You May Want To

Follow When Choosing Attire To Wear For Your Trip.

For Men:

Long Sleeves With Right Neck Tie

If You're Accustomed To Wearing A Simple Shirt Or Polo, You Have To Change It When You're Going To A Job Interview. You Have To Look Formal And Respectable So Wearing Long Sleeves And Necktie Will Make You Look Professional.

Slacks

Wearing Jeans Is A Big No-No For Job Interviews. Instead, Try To Wear Slacks Together With Your Long Sleeves Attire.

Black Leather Shoes

Rocking Your Leather Shoes On Your Interview Will Certainly Add Factor On Your Personality. Don't Forget To Wear Black Socks In Order To Look Clean And Tidy.

For Women:

Formal Top

White Long Sleeves And A Black Blazer As Cover Will Always Work. This Attire Will Make You Look Serious About Getting The Job You Are Applying For.

Slacks Or Pencil Skirt

The Skirt You Should Wear Must At Least Be Knee-Level High As You Don't Want To Look Too Sexy For Your Potential Employer. If You Want To Be Safer, Then Wear Slacks Instead.

High Heels But Not Too High

It Is Okay To Wear Shoes With Up To 2 Or 3 Inches Heels But Higher Than That Will Make You Look Like You Are Going To A Party Rather Than A Job Interview.

Light Make-Up

Putting Some Makeup Will Offer You A Livelier Appearance, But Do Not Put Too Much Bright Red Lipstick Or Thick Colorful Eye Shadow. Light Makeup Will Improve Your Overall Look.

These Are The Important Things That You Must Always Take Note Of When Going On A Job Interview. You Must Always Remember That You're Making The First Impression With Your Prospect Employer And Coworkers So Do Your Best. You Don't Need To Spend A Lot Of Money Buying A New Expensive Outfit, As Long As You Look

Neat, Professional, And Presentable, You Are Good To Go.

Chapter 4: Professional Etiquette And The Onsite Interview

"Be Sincere, Be Brief, Be Seated."- Franklin D. Roosevelt

During The Interview, Avoid Using Filler Words And Really Try To Get To The Point. Do Not Bull Shit Your Answers And Be Willing To Humbly Admit That You Do Not Know An Answer If You Do Not Know One. Avoid Referring To The Person As Bro, Man, Or Any Other Term You Have For Your Friends. Ladies Are Much Better About This As All Of Us Men Have That Inner Desire To Refer To Another Man As Anything But Their Name For Some Reason. I Personally Do Not Mind And Have Been Guilty Of Using, "Man" Here And There, But I Have Worked With Hiring Managers Who Have Ruled A Candidate Out For It. If In Person, Where A Suit Whether You Are Male Or Female. There Is No Other Look That Says You Care More And It Is Important. If You Wear The Suit, Shine The Shoes. Dull Shoes Make It Look

Like You Threw On Mom Or Dad's Old Suit They Have Not Used In Years Just To Check Off The Requirement And Did Not Care Enough To Buy $3 Shoe Shine To Make Your Shoes Look Presentable.

The More Detail Oriented You Are, The Better. Bring A Pad Folio With A Legal Pad Inside And Pen To Take Notes With. Have Written Out Questions Prepared Because You Will Not Remember Them By The Time You Are Asked If You Have Any.

Remember To Thank Anyone And Everyone Who Assists You In Any Way On The Company Premises. I Have Heard Of Stories Of The Hiring Manager Asking The Secretary If The Candidate Thanked Them On The Way Out.

After The Interview Is Over Be Sure To Send Over A Thank You Email Thanking The Interviewer For Their Time, Reiterating Your Interest, And Providing A Reference To Something You Spoke About And Why You Feel That Makes You A Good Fit For The Position. You Will Be 1 Out Of 500 Who Do This. I Did This After Each And Every Interview I Had And Am Blown

Away When A Candidate Does This After I Interview Them.

Chapter 5: Using Body Language

Welcome To The Final Chapter Of This Book. In This Chapter, We Will Discuss How You Can Effectively Use Your Body Language And Its Relevance In Job Interviews. You Speak With More Than Just Words. Your Body Speaks While You Are Not Paying Much Attention And You Unintentionally End Up Saying A Lot About Your Inner Emotions Through Your Body. Though It Is Purely Unintentional In Nature, You Can Learn To Master It, So As To Use It To Your Own Advantage In Job Interviews.

Facial Expressions

Your Face Says A Lot About You. Without Treading Into The Unsafe Field Of First Impressions, Your Face Is Your Entire Profile In An Interview. It Is The First Thing People Notice When You Walk Into The Room. Your Mind, Your Intellect, Your Wit, Your Sense Of Humor; All Come Secondary To The Onlookers' Minds. It Is Your Face That Leads Everything Else.

Droopy Eyes Clearly Indicate That The Person Is Not Interested In What Is In Front Of Him. It May, At Times, Even Be Offensive To Some People. On The Other Hand, Attentive And Alert Eyes Signify That You Are Genuinely Taking Interest What The Other Person Has To Say. However, Popping Out Eyes Is A Sign Towards Overacting. If A Person's Eyes Follows The Speaker's Hand Movement, Blink At The Right Time Intervals And Do Not Have Eye-Sand In Them, It Leaves Behind A Good Impression On The Speaker.

Watch Your Mouth. Literally! The Way You Position Your Lips In An Interview Is Vital Towards Indicating What Mood You Are In! If You Have An Open Mouth, It Shows That Either You Are Dumbfounded By The Conversation's Contents Or You Are Simply Sitting There Not Listening To Whatever's Being Said. On The Other Hand, If You Use Your Lips To Occasionally Smile A Little, It May Encourage The Interviewer To Do More Of What They Are Doing.

If You Are Twitching Your Lips, It Indicates That You Are Under A Bit Of Stress. Lip Twitching Has Always Been Associated With Nervousness. If You Twitch Your Lips In A Job Interview, Your Chances Of Getting Selected Drop Significantly, As It Shows A Lack Of Confidence.

Your Eyebrows Serve More Purpose Than Simply Completing Your Face. Use Them To Full Advantage To Show Inquisitiveness. You Can Focus Your Eyebrows Together To Signify That You Have Not Understood What Has Just Been Said. However, Too Much Of Squinting May Backfire, As It Will Be Overdoing It. You Can Show 'Surprise' By Raising Your Eyebrows, Despite A Certain English Idiom Appointing An Entirely Different Interpretation To 'Raising Eyebrows.' Express Shock Or Mild Surprise By Exploiting Your Eyebrows Smartly.

Your Facial Expressions Cover More Than Just Your Eyes, Lips And Eyebrows. It Is How Your Face As A Whole Is Presented That Matters And Not Just Its Individual Parts. When You Have A Smiling Face, It Is

Natural That Those Sitting Right Across The Interview Table Feel Good Vibes Coming From You. On The Other Hand, A Face With A Grimace On It Is Considered Cold And Unfriendly.

Body Postures

Body Postures Are All About How You Carry Yourself. It Is The Ultimate Platform For Your Body Language To Be Displayed In Full Vigor.

Sitting Is As Important As Walking. Do Not Pull The Chair Out And Just Assume That You Are To Sit Unless Someone Asks You To. It Is Not Only Against Your Prospects Of Landing A Job, But Also Rude To Sit Down On Your Own As It Gives Off An Aura Of Superiority. Wait For One Of The Interviewers To Ask You To Sit. Assume A Straight Posture, With Your Backbone Touching The Back Of The Chair At All Points. Do Not Sit Too Stiff, As That Could Lead To Cramps And Make You Nervous Eventually.

Do Not Sit Slouching. Straighten Up Your Shoulders A Bit And Appear Smart While Doing So. Do Not Cross Your Legs Under

The Table. Though Most Interviewers Cannot See What Is Going On Under The Table, That Position Does Affect Your Upper Body. One Can Easily Tell How Casually Your Legs Are Placed Under The Table By Taking A Single Glance At Your Upper Body.

Do Not Place One Leg Above The Other While Sitting. It Shows That You Are Not Just Confident About Yourself, But Also Show A General Attitude Of Carelessness Towards The Interviewers. Behave In A Manner That Sends The Message That You Respect Them.

Sitting Upright In An Interview Might Go In Favor Of You Since It Displays An Attentive Mentality. On The Other Hand, Adopting A Slouching Position Signifies That You Are In The Mood To Hear Them Out And Are Only There Only To Doodle And Pass Time.

Gestures

In An Interview, If You Are Sitting In A Cross-Armed Position, It Implies That You Are Not Welcome To Others' Point Of Views And Ideas. It Displays A Cold Attitude And Often Does Not Come Off As

Desirable. On The Other Hand, Instead Of Crossing Arms, If You Sit With Your Hands In Your Lap Or On The Table, You Give Off A Friendly And Warmer Aura And It Will Definitely Fetch You Brownie Points.

It Is A Sign Of Careless Confidence To Casually Fling Your Arms Around While Walking. On The Other Hand, If You Clench Your Fists And Walk, It May Imply That You Are Calculated And Reserved About Yourself.

In Certain Countries, Finger Gestures Can Be Interpreted In Several Ways. The Majority Of Our Planet Follows The Rule Of Showing The Middle Finger To Be Offensive. On The Other Hand, In Some Parts Of The World, It's The Display Of Index Finger That's Considered Aggressive And Offensive.

Hands Can Be Used To Convey Emotions Too. Joining Your Hands In A Namaste Sign Shows That You Mean Respect Towards The Person. Bowing Down Is Another Form Of Respect Followed By The Japanese. If You Show Someone The 'Thumbs Up' Sign, It Means That You Are Either Wishing

Them Good Luck Or Are Conveying 'Okay' Or One Of Its Variants. However, If You Do The Same In Other Countries Like Iran Or Thailand; It Can Be Taken As An Equivalent Of Showing The Middle Finger In The West.

So, Make Sure You Do Not Consciously Or Subconsciously Offend Your Interviewers With Your Body Language Or Gestures.

Handshakes

A Very Common Way To Greet Each Other Is By Shaking Each Other's Hand. This Has Been A Tradition Since The Medieval Period. A Handshake Is Supposed To Signify Greeting, Completion, Agreement Or Friendship And Calling Off Of War.

In An Interview, The First And Only Physical Interaction You Will Have With Your Prospective Employer Is Through The Handshake That You Perform When You First Walk In. The Way A Person Shakes His Hand With Others Says A Lot About Him. If The Handshake Is Firm, It Means The Person Performing It Is Confident And Is Clear About His Intentions.

On The Other Hand, If It's A Loose Handshake, It Displays A Lack Of Self-Confidence And Casualness. A Weak Handshake Is Often Taken To Be A Sign Towards Half-Agreement And Not A Full Nod. Studies Over The Years Have Classified Handshakes Into Various Categories Like The Bone Crusher – Squeezing Hands Too Hard, And The Limp Fish-Weakly Done Handshake.

Miscellaneous

Biting Your Nails Is A Clear Sign Of Anxiety. Though It Is Perfectly Human To Be Anxious, Remember It Is A Rat Race Competition Out There. Interviewers Will Be Hunting For People That Are Not Going Through Their Own Personal Issues Already. Hence, It Is Advisable Not To Bite Your Nails And Give Them A Chance To Strike Your Name Off The List.

Do Not Nod Or Shake Your Head At The Wrong Times. In A Fit Of Frenzy And A Rush To Impress, Many Candidates Fail To Even Grasp The Question And Simply Nod Or Shake Their Head. A Nod Signifies Yes And A Mere Shaking Of Head Denotes No.

If You Have Fully Understood The Question And Are Clear And Ready To Elucidate, Only Then Must You Nod Or Shake Your Head. Nodding And Shaking Of The Head Also Comes Under Body Language And Must Be Sparingly Used.

Do Not Flinch At A Question That Has Caught You Unaware. It Is Perfectly Fine For A Candidate To Come Across Questions That Might Baffle Them From The Very Beginning. However, Do Not Make Any Gesture That Says, 'I Am Not Liking This Question And I Hate You For Asking It." Instead Of Flinching Or Making A Face, Act Curious And Tell Them That You Have No Idea Regarding The Question's Answer And Would Like To Know The Same.

Tell Them That You Give Up Despite Trying Hard, And Ask If They Could Give You The Right Answer. Such A Gesture Puts You In A Good Light. It Shows That You Have The Thirst For Knowledge.

Make Sure Your Feet Are Positioned Properly. Feet That Are Placed In The Direction Of The Door Paint A Very Sorry

Picture Of A Candidate. It Indicates That The Candidate Is Not Very Keen On Bagging The Job And Is Sitting There Just For The Sake Of Appearing At The Job Interview. It Also Shows That You Are Ready To Walk Out Any Moment The Interview Is Over Which Is Obviously Not A Healthy Sign.

Overview

When Called For An Interview, Make Yourself Presentable. A Fat Belly Becomes Presentable When Accompanied By A Well-Fitting And Ironed Somber Professionalism-Oriented Shirt And The Right Set Of Pants. Trim, Shave And Wash Before Walking In For The Interview. Maintain A Good Posture And Talk In A Polite Manner.

Confidence Can Be Improved By How You Look But Don't Overdo It. Show Them That You Are A Team Person And Are Willing To Take Up Leadership Positions When Asked To. If Asked Something That Flips You Out, Instead Of Freaking Out, Stay Calm And Honestly Tell Them You Have No Idea. Do Not Overdo The Way You Speak And Just

Talk How You Would Normally Talk With Your Friends. Impress Them With Your Logical Clarity, Communication Skills And Technical Know-How That Are Pre-Requisites For The Job.

Chapter 6: Cover Letter – Your Grand Entrance

One Thing Sorely Lacking In The Many Resumes I've Received Is A Cover Letter. Your Cover Letter Is Your Introduction, Or Your Grande Entrée. It Is A Way For You To Give The Potential Employer A Taste Of Who You Are As A Person. You've Put Together An Impressive Professional Document That Gives The Employer An Idea Of Your Work Ethic And Experience, But This Is Your Chance To Explain Why You Want Or Deserve The Position.

You Want To Write The Cover Letter With Professionalism, But Also Find A Way To Make Yourself Stand Out From The Rest Of The Resumes. While You Can Also Find Generic Templates For Cover Letters With A Simple Google Search, Keep In Mind That The Templates Are So General That Anyone Can Plug Their Information In And Use Them. The Goal Of Your Cover Letter Is To Give The Employer A Glimpse Into Your Personality. You Could Start The

Cover Letter With A Favorite Quote That Is Applicable To The Position, Or A Shocking Statement That Intrigues The Reader. Think Of A Creative Way To Catch Your Reader's Attention.

Employers Like To See Cover Letters Because Offices Have Certain Dynamics. If You Are Applying For A Smaller Company, It Will Be Important That Your Personality Fits Well With Those Already Working In That Office. I Worked In An Office Of Six Employees Where Everyone Was Friendly, But When It Came To Work, Everyone Was So Focused That The Office Stayed Pretty Quiet. We Decided To Hire A New Person Into The Office And Though Her Qualifications For The Position Were Applicable, We Soon Came To Find Out That This New Hire Was A Chatterbox. Every Day She Would Share Personal Stories From Home Or Talk About A Work Situation That She Either Found Humorous Or Annoying. Even Though We Would Have Freely Listened To Her In A Different Environment, The Office Setting Was Too Fast Paced And Busy For Anyone To Return

The Conversation. In Fact, It Would Often Just Distract From The Sense Of Urgency That Needed To Be A Part Of The Business Day. It Is So Important For Companies To Find That Perfect Fit, So They Can Move The Goals Of The Company Forward Quickly And Efficiently. A Cover Letter Can Provide The Small Insight Needed To Assure The Company That You Are That Perfect Fit.

Another Reason Employers Like To See A Cover Letter Is That It Gives The Whole Hiring Process A Touch Of Humanity. Reading Resume After Resume Can Become Exhausting, But A Fresh Cover Letter Brings Life From The Page. Instead Of Looking At A Page Of Words, The Employer Can Look At Reflections Of The Candidates' Minds.

Impress Them With Your Wit

When I First Met My Husband, I Decided To Read Up And Study Everything I Could About His Craft: Motocross. I Looked Up Everything From Different Race Teams To How To Build A Motor For The Bike, And On Each Date Had A New Piece Of

Information To Throw Out And Blow His Mind. It Worked...We're Married.

In The Same Way, Impress Your Potential Employers. Your Cover Letter Should Touch On One Or Two Things The Company Has Accomplished, Or Praise The Way Their Operation Works. Show Your Interest In The Company, Not Just The Job Position. Employers Want To Hire Someone That Is Invested In The Company And Who Isn't Just Looking For The Next Paycheck. Let Them Know That Your Interests Align With The Company's Ambitions. Show That By Choosing You, The Company Can Grow While Investing In A Successful Future.

Be Charming

While Putting All The Right Pieces Together For Your Cover Letter, Top It Off With Some Charisma. Win Your Reader Over With Your Charm. If You Have A Humorously Sarcastic Personality, Write Something That Will Make Your Reader Smile. If You Have A Gentle Spirit, Appeal To The Reader's Compassionate Side. Keep Your Audience In Mind As Well As The Fact

That Your Reader Will Have Many Letters And Resumes To Go Through. Strive To Put An Abundance Of Quality In A Small Quantity Of Words.

Chapter 7: Do Your Research

"What Is The One Thing About Our Company That Really Attracted You To Come And Apply With Us?"

Researching All You Can About The Company Is A Very Important Part Of The Job Interview Process As It Lets You Sell Yourself Perfectly On Why You Make For A Great Fit Within The Organization. If It Turns Out That You Don't Have Much Knowledge About The Company, The Recruiter Will Be Immediately Put Off. That's Because He Will Think That You Either Don't Care About The Job And The Company Enough To Bother To Research It, Or He Might Assume That You Do Not Have A Good Work Ethic Because You Could Not Do Something As Simple As A Quick Internet Search.

Moreover, Can You Be Confident That You Are The Right Person To Fill In The Position When You Have Not Done Any Kind Of Homework On What The Organization Is All About And What They Deal In? Nobody

Is Asking You To Memorize Every Single Detail Regarding The Profile Of The Organization. However, Spending Twenty To Thirty Minutes Browsing Through Their Website – Special Focus Should Be Given To The "About Us" Section – As Well As The Latest News Pertaining To The Company Can Prove To Be A Smart Decision.

First Impressions Are Lasting Impressions
Every Small Detail Should Be Looked Upon As An Opportunity To Create A Positive Initial Impression. As The Old Adage Goes, "First Impressions Are Often The Last Impressions!" A Great Tactic To Employ Is Asking The Interviewer Questions About Certain Initiatives Going On In The Organization, Which Highlights Your Interest And The Research You Have Done On The Company.

You Could Say Something Like, "I Noticed How Much Your Company Tends To Focus On Giving Back To The Community Through Numerous Programs. Could You Please Share A Little More On These Things?" Not Only Does This Show The

Kind Of Interest You Take Towards The Organization, But Also Puts You Forward As A Person Who Is Actively Looking To Contribute And Learn New Things.

While In An Interview, There Are Not Many Things That You Get To Enjoy Complete Control Over, But Doing Your Due Diligence In Researching The Organization Before The Interview Is Certainly Something That Is Entirely In Your Own Hands. You Can Make The Most Of Your Knowledge And Put Your Best Foot Forward, Which Will Go A Long Way In Impressing The Recruiter And Put You In A Better Position To Land The Job.

Highlight Your Skills And Experience That Are Potentially Valuable To The Company

To Start With, You Should Be Aware Of The Criteria That Make An Individual Qualify As A Suitable Candidate For The Organization. This Is Your Opportunity To Portray Yourself As Someone Who Is Best Suited For This Position. Carefully Read Through The Job Posting To See Exactly What Kind Of Candidate They Are Looking For.

The Careers Page (As Well As The About Us And Corporate Values Pages) Of The Employing Organization Is Also A Good Place To Gather Information On The Kind Of Employee The Organization Desires. You Could Also Reach Out To People Who Are Already Employed With The Company And Ask About The Things That The Management Places Maximum Value On Inside The Workplace.

Get To Know The Organization's Key Members

People Who Are Important And Integral To An Organization Are Ideally Those Employees Who Have Been Trusted With Important Positions Within The Establishment. These People Could Include Department Directors And Managers, As Well As Top Executives Such As The Ceo And Vice-Presidents.

Once Again, The About Us Page Will Give You All The Information You Need. You Can Also Go Through The Employee Bios To Gather More Knowledge. Following Them On Linkedin And Twitter Is Another Good Option To Learn What These People

Say About The Organization And What Kind Of Values They Represent.

Learn About News And Recent Developments At The Company

While Going For A Job Interview, You Need To Have Complete Knowledge About The Latest Updates And News Of What Is Going On Inside The Organization. On Most Company Websites, You Will Come Across A Page That Is Dedicated Exclusively To News Events And Press Releases. This Proves To Be A Great Source Where You Can Come Across Information Regarding The Latest Updates And News In A Company.

Get Familiar With The Organization's Values, Mission, And Culture

As A Job Seeker, You Should Be Confident About Highlighting How You Are A Good Fit In The Company Culture. In A Study For Millennial Branding, It Was Found That As Many As 43 Percent Of Hr Professionals Give Superior Importance To A Good Cultural Fit Which They See As One Of The Most Important Qualities In Job Seekers

Who Send Forth Their Applications For Suitable Openings.

While Doing Research On The Employer, You Should Also Pay Close Attention To Everything That Is Written On The Company Website Regarding Their Mission And Values. Another Way You Can Pick Up More Information On The Kind Of Culture Prevailing Inside The Organization Is By Following Its Various Social Media Accounts.

Find Out More About Clients, Products, And Services

If You Are Going To Think Of Yourself As A Potential Employee Within The Organization, You Need To Develop An Idea On The Kind Of Work You Will Be Asked To Do Upon Being Hired.

Knowing Your Company's Clients And Target Markets, And The Kind Of Services And Products They Offer Will Help You In Your Interview Because You Will Be Able To Better Highlight How Exactly You Will Be Able To Contribute To The Company And Its Goals.

Try To Get Some Inside Information

Another Thing That Can Help You Prepare For Your Job Interview Is Find Out More About How The Company Treats Its Employees. There Are Websites Which Can Be Of Immense Help To Job Seekers In Helping Them Discover More Inside Information About A Company That Is Not Usually Available On Their Business Website.

These Websites, Such As Glassdoor, Give You Detailed Information On Topics Such As The Hiring Process, Company Reviews, Employee Duties And Functions, And Salary Figures.

Learn More About The Person Interviewing You

If It Is Possible, Try And Find Out Who Will Be Interviewing You. This Can Turn Out To Be An Advantage By Giving You A Better Chance Of Making A Fruitful Connection With The Individual Which Can Also Help You Engage In More Meaningful Conversations.

Finding Out Who This Person Is Who Is Going To Take Your Interview May Not Prove To Be The Easiest Thing To Do.

However, A Little Bit Of Investigation Should Help You Locate His/Her Name. The Email That You Had Received Regarding A Call For This Interview Should Be Your First Point Of Contact. If You Are Not Able To Find This Information In The Email, Send A Polite Reply To Ask About The Person Who Is Likely To Be The Interviewer.

Once You Have This Name In Your Possession, Look The Person Up On Twitter Or Linkedin. This Will Help You Get A Background On The Interviewer As Well As The Position He Or She Holds Inside The Company. You May Also Chance Upon Some Common Point Of Interest Between The Two Of You That You Can Bring Into Your Discussion During The Interview.

The Top Sources For Company Research

If You Want To Get Hired, Always Do Your Due Diligence And Research The Company You Are Applying For. When You Go In For An Interview Well-Informed And Confident About How You Can Contribute, It Can Really Set You Apart From Other

Prospective Candidates. Here Are Ten Of The Best Resources For Finding Out More About Your Potential Future Employer:

Official Company Website

It Goes Without Saying That Your First And Best Source Of Information On The Company Is Its Own Website. Spending An Hour Reading Through A Company's Website Can Give You A Wealth Of Information On Its Corporate Philosophy, Careers And Job Postings At The Organization, Future Plans And Outlooks, Current Investment Strategy, All The Latest News On Investments, Executive Team Members And Their Biographies, And Corporate Social Responsibility Initiatives.

Google

Certainly, What Better Place To Kick-Start Your Research Than The Grandmaster Of All Things Under The Sun, Google? While Personal Contacts Inside The Organization You Are Looking For Can Certainly Be Of Considerable Help, The World's Most Popular Search Engine Will Let You Access A Wealth Of Information At Your

Convenience. Aside From Finding Out More About The Organization Itself, Doing An Online Search Can Also Show You Competitors As Well As The State Of The Industry In General.

Linkedin

Linkedin Allow You To Follow The Company's Official Page, And A Little Searching Will Also Show You The Pages Of Employees Currently Or Previously Associated With This Organization. Linkedin Is Home To A Wealth Of Information On People Moving In And Out Of Companies, Where They Are Coming From Or Where They Are Going To, Job Openings Available, Employee Benefits, Company Services And Their Products, As Well As Some Of The Common Qualifications And Skills Of The Current Employees.

Twitter And Facebook

Numerous Companies Also Set Up Their Corporate Pages On Social Networking Sites Such As Facebook And Twitter Which Turn Out To Be Important Sources For All The Latest Happenings And News.

Twitter Comes In Handy For Following Conversations Regarding The Overall Company Culture, New Products, And Job Openings Within The Organization. Wal-Mart, Ge, Bank Of America, And Google Are Among The Companies That Boast Robust Career Pages On Twitter.

It Has Also Become Increasingly Fashionable For Companies To Hire From Facebook With Job Opening Posts On Their Fan Pages. Facebook Can Also Be Used In Market Research For Floating Ideas Regarding New Services And Products Because Of Its Engaging And Interactive Nature.

Company Blogs

With Content Marketing Continuing To Become More Important These Days, Companies Of All Sizes Have Set Up Blogs Which Feature Well-Crafted Messages Regarding The Latest News, Mission And Focus Of The Company In Question. You Can Also Get An Insight Into The Personality And Culture Of The Company Through These Blogs.

Financial Statements And Annual Reports

For Publicly Traded Companies, Financial Statements And Annual Reports Are Excellent Information Sources For Analyzing Their Current Performance As Well As Forecasting How They Will Do In The Future. Typically, These Documents Can Be Found Under The Investor Information Section Of A Public Company Website. If You Can Afford To Wait, You Can Also Request A Copy To Be Mailed To Your Home.

Press Releases

Whenever They Want To Make An Official Announcement, Either Regarding A New Company Policy, A Product Release, Or Just General News, A Company Or Its Public Relations Firm Will Send Out A Press Release. Look For A Company's Latest Press Releases, As Some Of This Information May Still Be So New That It Has Not Been Updated On Their Website Or Documents.

Industry Associations

While They May Not Have Any Data Specific To The Company You Are Applying For, Industry Associations Are A Great

Resource For Information As Well. By Reading Up On The Latest Trends In The Industry Where The Company Is Operating, You Will Be Able To Tell If Things Are Currently Going Well And Whether They Will Continue To Be Great Down The Road.

For Example, If The Company You Are Applying For Deals In A Fast-Growing Segment Like Solar Technology, Then There Is Potential For Growth For Your Career If You Are Hired.

Competitors

Never Forget To Run A Research On The Companies That Are Direct Competitors To Your Target Organization. Find Out What Kind Of Products Or Services They Offer, And How They Are Different (Or Similar) To The Company You Are Applying For. It Will Give The Interviewer A Positive Impression If You Show An Awareness Of The Competition And Offer Thoughts On How The Company Can Improve And Gain More Market Share From Its Rivals.

Glassdoor

A Site That Can Be Freely Described As An Anonymous Workplace Community, Glassdoor Allows You To Enjoy A Free Inside View At Over 200,000 Businesses Complete With Interview Questions, Employee Reviews, And Salaries.

This Comprehensive Resource Has Become The Best Choice For Researching Companies Since The Reviews Are Coming From Actual Employees Who Also Give A List Of The Pros And Cons Associated With Working For That Organization. Salary Expectations Can Be Identified And Interview Preparations Can Be Made By Seeing Actual Interview Questions That Have Been Put Forward To Other Candidates In The Past.

Chapter 8: The Appropriate Way To Appear For An Interview

When You Go To A Job Interview You Are Dressing To Impress Your Future Boss. You May Spend Money Investing In A New Business Suit That You Are Hoping You Will Soon Be Wearing To Your New Job. Even With The Best Suit You Can Sometimes Encounter Pitfalls That Even The Most Experienced Job Seekers Can Fall Into. You Could Fail Your Job Interview And Not Know Why If You Are Not Aware Of These Pitfalls That May Arise.

If For Example You Have Sweaty Hands And You Are Not Even Aware Of This Because You Have Your Mind On Preparing For Your Interview. As Soon As You Shake Hands With Your Future Boss With A Cold Sweaty Hand, He Is Going To Translate That Into You Being A Person That Lacks Self-Confidence, Not The Kind Of Person He Wants On His Team. Right Then And There You Have Lost Your Chance At This Job. Let's Face It Most People Are Not Too

Fond Of Getting A Wet And Sticky Hand Shake. This Is Something That Does Not Make A Good First Impression.

You May Feel That A Wet Hand, Or A Wrinkled Shirt, And Uncombed Hair Are Very Trivial Things. You Believe That Your Superb Skill Set And Solid Background Is Enough To Ensure That You Will Be Hired.

The Problem Is If The Future Employer Doesn't Like Your Attitude That Comes Out In The Sloppy Way You Present Yourself, They Are Not Going To Hire You, They Will Go With Someone Else.

It Can Be Very Hard At Times For Interviewers To Decide On What Candidate To Hire. Sometimes They Will Resort To Basic Tactics By Eliminating The Candidate Who Looked Tired. If For Example You Had To Work A Long Shift Before Your Interview It May Be Worth Your While To Mention To Your Interviewer That Is Why You Look So Tired During The Interview. You May Get The Job Because Your Future Employer Is Fair And Reasonable And Was Understanding Of Your Situation. If You Do Not Explain

Why You Look Tired They May Go With Someone Else.

Importance Of First Impression

Many Experts Have Stressed That The First Impression Is Very Crucial When Trying To Make A Good Impression To Others Such As Future Boss. The Best Way For You To Give A Good Impression To Your Future Boss Is To Make Sure That You Are Dressed Well And Groomed For The Interview.

Dressing Appropriately At Your Interview Is Important Because Not Only Will Your Future Boss Be Deciding If He Wants To Hire You, But Future Teammates Will Be Giving You The Once Over. Future Teammates Will Be Deciding If You Are Someone They Will Want To Work With.

These Decisions Will Be Based On Your Appearance During Your Interview. The Teammates Will Be Spending One Third Of Their Life With You So There Is No Way That They Will Pick Up Someone They Do Not Like.

The Truth Is Once You Are At The Point Of Being Chosen For An Interview, The Other

Candidates Will Have Similar Skill Sets Making Not Much Difference Between You. Therefore, When It Comes To Small Things Like Your Personal Appearance This Is Going To Have A Critical Effect On Your Future Employee Deciding Whether To Hire You Or Not. It May Boil Down To Something As Simple As They Liked The Color Choice Of Tie You Wore To The Interview. Perhaps Your Tie Had Their Company Logo Colors In It.

Don't Have To Spend A Small Fortune

Don't Think That In Order To Make A Good Impression During An Interview That You Must Go Out And Spend A Small Fortune On Clothing, And A New Hairstyle And Cut. It Is Not Necessary That You Add To Your Credit Card Bill At A Time When You Should Be Watching Your Spending Especially If You Are Out Of Work. You Do Not Want To Go Overboard Where You End Up Looking Like A Person That Does Not Belong On The Team Of The Future Boss That You Are Trying To Impress.

If For Example You Are A Lady You Do Not Want To Apply At A Financial Institution

Wearing A Sheer Low-Cut Blouse, Mini Skirt And Big High Heels, Looking More Like A Fashion Sexy Model. You Want To Try And Blend Into The Crowd That You Will Be Working Besides, You Will Have A Much Better Chance Of Getting The Job If You Look Like You Will Fit In With Their Team.

Perfume During An Interview

You Love To Wear Perfume It Is Great At Showing Off Your Personality, Style, And Taste. Who Isn't Wearing Perfume, And Who Doesn't Love Perfume.

When It Comes To A Job Interview You Must Be Very Careful With Your Perfume During A Job Interview. Make Sure That You Wear Only A Small Amount. Remember That You Are Going To Be In An Enclosed Room For At Least Forty Minutes. If You Are Wearing Strong Perfume This May Put Your Future Boss Off, It May Cause Them To Feel Poorly.

The Worse Thing That Could Happen Is That Your Future Boss Is Allergic To The Type Of Perfume That You Are Wearing. If This Happens Then You Can Be Sure That

Your Interview Is Going To Be Over In A Flash.

You Don't Want To Wear The Same Perfume That Your Boss's Ex Used To Wear, You Could Be Out The Door Because Your Choice Of Perfume Brought Forth Bad Memories For Your Boss.

Go With A Subtle Nice Smell

It Is Very Important That You Smell Nice And Fresh When Going Into Your Interview, While At The Same Time You Are Not Overwhelming Your Boss With Strong Perfume.

A Lady Should Wear Only A Bit Of Scented Lotion Or Perfume. Don't Put The Perfume On Just Before Your Interview This Will Make It Smell Too Strong.

A Man Should Use A Very Light Touch Of Cologne Or Aftershave.

Make Sure That Your Breath Is Fresh When You Walk Into Your Interview. Do Not Chew Gum Or Be Sucking On Mints During The Interview.

Chapter 9: How To Create Cover Letters That Get Great Results

You've Probably Heard The Story Of The Guy Who Visits His Doctor Complaining Of Pain In His Eye Every Time He Drinks Hot Cocoa. After Asking A Few Questions, The Doc Offers This Solution: "Take The Spoon Out Of Your Cup When You Drink." When It Comes To Creating Cover Letters, Most Job Searchers Make The Process Much More Painful Than It Needs To Be. In This Chapter, I'll Show You How To "Take The Spoon Out Of Your Cup" To Easily Create Effective Cover Letters That Get Great Results.

Set Up Your Letter Professionally

Your Cover Letter And Resume Go Hand In Hand In Representing You As A Qualified Candidate. For This Reason, It's Important To Present Your Cover Letter As Professionally As You Do Your Resume. Often, You Can Easily Create Your Header By Copying And Pasting The Header From Your Resume. Be Sure To Include Your

Name Or Initials, As Well As Your Phone Number And E-Mail Information. Your Address Is Optional, Especially If You Want To Maintain Your Confidentiality; However, If You Don't Include Your Address, At Least Include Some Regional Information.

Enter The Date And Employer Info (Including A Contact Name If Possible)

The Type Of Information You Include In The Employer's Address And Your Salutation Will Depend On The Opportunity. For Instance, If You're Responding To A Blind Ad, It's Likely That You Won't Have A Contact Name Or Address. In This Case, Just List The Information You Do Have, Such As, "Attention Human Resources, Re: Accounting Specialist Position."

If It's Not A Blind Ad, And A Company Name Or Address Is Provided, I Encourage You To Research More Details About The Company Using The Internet, Or By Calling The Company Directly, Aiming To Find Out The Name Of The Hiring Manager.

Note: Unless You're Applying For A Position Within The Human Resources Department, The Human Resources Manager Is Not The Hiring Manager. The Hiring Manager Is The Person You Would Report To...In Other Words, Your Future Boss. Although It Makes Sense To Submit Your Application Materials To Human Resources, It's Also Highly Effective To Send A Second Copy Of Your Materials To The Hiring Manager. Including The Name (Properly Spelled, Of Course!) Of This Person Can Go A Long Way Toward Helping Your Application Materials To Stand Out From The Competition. A Quick Call To The Company Asking, "Who Is In Charge Of The X Department," (Filling In The X With The Function Appropriate To Your Job Search Focus) Is Often All It Takes To Get This Valuable Piece Of Data. If You're Not Able To Obtain The Name Of A Contact Person, The Greeting, "Dear Hiring Manager" Is Really Not Great. In Our Job Ads, We Will State, "Please Address Your Application To Helen Wells "For Example. It Is Quite Astounding Then When At Least

Half Of The Applicants Address Their Letter To "The Hiring Manager" Or "To Whom It May Concern." Come On, Really Now?

Begin Your Letter With A To-The-Point First Paragraph

The Following Starter Paragraph, Customized With Specifics Relevant To Your Opportunity, Is A Great Way To Begin Your Letter.

Your Job Advert, For An Account Executive Dated 1 September On Www.Gumtree.Com Refers. Herewith Please Find My Brief Resume. I Know That I Can Add Great Value To Your Company As I Am A Hard Worker, Get Great Results And Am A Team Player. I Would Love To Work For Www.Brandinnovation.Co.Za. I Have Done A Lot Of Research On Your Company. I Have Heard Great Reports In The Industry And Would Consider It A Privilege To Work For You. Following Is A Summary Of My Qualifications As They Pertain To Your Position Requirements:

Additionally, If You Have The Name Of A Mutual Acquaintance Who Has Referred

You, The First Paragraph Is The Ideal Place To Include This Information.

List Three Bullets Highlighting The Most Important Aspects Of Your Background

For The Main Part Of Your Cover Letter, Choose Three Pieces Of Information About You That Are Most Relevant To The Company's Priorities, And Highlight Them With Bullets. Often, You Can Determine Its Primary Needs From The Job Ad, Or Based On Your Own Knowledge Of The Position.

Worried About Choosing The "Right" Three Points To Cover With Your Bullet Statements? Try Not To Sweat This Step Too Much. Just Pick The Three That You Feel Are Most Important, And Resist The Urge To Address Everything About Your Background In The Cover Letter. It's Too Much For The Hiring Manager Or Resume Screener To Wade Through! (Never Lose Sight Of The Fact That Screeners Might Be Reviewing 100 Or More Applications...Make Their Jobs Easy For Them!)

Conclude Your Letter With Proposed Next Steps

Now That The Resume Screener Is Excited About What You Have To Offer Based On The Three Highlighted Bullet Statements You Provided, Tell Him What You Aim To Have Happen Next —Specifically, To Review Your Resume, Have You In For An Interview, Or To Expect Your Call:

Additional Details About My Background Are Provided On The Enclosed Resume. I Would Welcome The Opportunity To Talk With You Further About The Job Title Position And How I Might Benefit Your Organization In This Role. In The Next Few Days, I Will Follow Up With You To Confirm Receipt Of These Materials, And To Determine A Logical Next Step.

You Might Be Thinking, "This Cover Letter Format Seems Too 'Light.' Shouldn't I Be Including Statements About My Character, Such As My Work Ethic And Loyalty?" Good Question, And The Answer Is...In General, No. Why? Because It's Very Difficult To Describe Your Positive Qualities In A Few Sentences And Have Them Come Across Clearly And Sincerely. (Be Honest...You've Tried This Before,

Haven't You? And It Most Likely Didn't Go Well.) For Example, Consider The Statement, "I Am A Hard Worker And Devoted To Going The Extra Mile To Get The Job Done." Most People, When They Read A Statement Like This, Think To Themselves, "Yeah? Prove It..." Rather Than, "Oh, Goody...A Hardworking, Extra-Mile Kinda Guy!" Another Reason Not To Include Difficult-To-Prove Statements About Your Character Is That Most Other Job Searchers Are Attempting To Do The Same Thing. So Instead Of Saying You're An Awesome Person, Show It In Your Cover Letter By Including A Few Powerful Pieces Of Evidence.

Although Writing Effective Resumes And Cover Letters Is An Important Activity, It Certainly Doesn't Deserve To Receive The Majority Of Your Job Search Effort.

By Using A Proven Approach To Creating Cover Letters, Requiring You To Invest A Minimum Of Time And Effort, You Will Be Able To Achieve More Of What You Want In Your Job Search And Career.

Writing Effective Letters To Support Your Job Search Can Seem Overwhelming. How Do You Communicate Your Best Qualities In A Concise, Compelling Letter, While Also Motivating The Decision Maker To Call You For An Interview? Yikes—What Pressure! Rather Than Make Yourself Crazy Attempting To Achieve This Near-Impossible Feat, It Makes Sense To Stick With A Proven Approach, Devoting Your Time To Filling In The Details That Are Relevant To You. Will It Feel Strange, Trying A Different Approach? Probably...But Give It A Go, And See How It Works For You.

Chapter 10: Dealing With Interview Questions: Possible Questions To Expect And Questions To Ask

Questions You Should Expect From The Interviewer

It Would Be Nice If You Were Aware Of The Exact Questions The Interviewer Will Be Asking You In The Next Interview. Although It Is Not Possible For You To Read Minds, You Can Increase Your Confidence Level By Knowing Some Of The Possible Questions You Should Expect In An Interview. Before Reading Some Of The Questions, I Highly Recommend That You Abstain From Having A Rehearsed Response To The Interview Questions.

Instead, Focus On Being Comfortable With The Questions You Might Be Asked And The Things Interviewers Are Searching For In Your Response. There Are Hundreds Of Possible Questions You Should Expect, Depending On Your Industry, But Consider Some Of The Possible Questions Below.

Tell Me A Little About Yourself - We Have Already Talked About This Vital Interview Question. Avoid Providing A Complete History Of Your Employment, Just Offer A Pitch, Which Is Concise And Compelling And Will Prove That You Are Suited For The Job.

Tell Me How You Heard About The Job - This Is An Excellent Chance For You To Stand Out And Display Your Passion For Connecting With The Hiring Company. Share What Specifically Attracted You To The Position When You First Saw The Job Posting.

What Do You Know About The Company? Remember I Earlier Discussed How To Research The Hiring Company. Now Is The Chance To Use The Information You Obtained From Your Research. The Interviewer Desires To Know If You Genuinely Care About The Company. Therefore, You Can Make A Statement Such As "I'm Personally Attracted To The Company Values Because..."

Why Do You Want This Job? The Hiring Manager Wants To Find Out If You Are Passionate About The Job. To Answer This Question, You Need To Identify Critical Things That Make The Role The Best For You And Share Why You Love The Company.

Tell Me About Your Most Significant Professional Strengths - You Need To Be Accurate When Answering This Question. Avoid Talking About The Strengths The Interviewer Desires To Hear, But Your Real Strengths. Your Strengths Should Be Relevant To The Position, And It Should Be Specific. For Instance, Instead Of Using "People Skills" Which Is Commonly Used, You Can Choose "Relationship Building". Make Sure You Provide An Example Of How You Demonstrated The Traits You Mentioned In A Professional Setting.

What Are Your Weaknesses? The Interviewer Is Attempting To Identify The Key "Red Flags" In Your Life And Estimate Your Self-Awareness And Honesty. Do Not Give A Response Like "Nothing! I'm Perfect", Preferably, Provide A Response

Of Something You Struggle With Which You Are Attempting To Improve.

Tell Me About Your Most Significant Professional Achievement - The Best Way To Be Hired Is To Provide A Track Record Of Results And Accomplishments. So, Make Use Of The Star Approach; Set Up The Situation And Task You Were Expected To Complete. Spend More Time Talking About What You Actually Did (Action) To Handle The Task And Finally Talk About The Results You Achieved.

Tell Me About A Difficult Issue You Encountered At Work And How Did You Resolve It? The Hiring Manager Wants To Know How You Will Respond To Conflict. What Happens If You Are Hired? You Can Still Make Use Of The Star Method In Answering The Question And Focus On How You Professionally And Productively Handled The Situation. Remember, It Has To Be A Happy Ending.

Tell Me About Your Dream Job - The Hiring Manager Wants To Find Out If The Position You Are Applying For Is In Sync With Your Ultimate Career Goals, So, Your Response

Would Align With The Information You Obtained About The Company During Your Research.

Are You Interviewing With Other Companies? Of Course, The Interviewer Wants To Know If You Are Serious About The Industry. One Of The Best Approaches Is To Mention That You Are Presently Exploring Similar Options In The Industry. You Can Say That All The Companies You Are Applying To Have A Common Characteristic, Which Is The Chance To Use Some Skills, And Critical Abilities You Have.

So Why Do You Want To Leave Your Current Job? One Of The Things You Should Never Do Is To Make Negative Remarks About Your Previous Job Or Employer. Your Response Should Signify That You Are Eager To Accept New Opportunities And That You Learned A Lot While Working At Your Current Job.

Other Possible Questions You Might Expect Are:

What Is Your Ideal Work Environment?
What Do You Expect In A New Role?
So, Why Were You Fired?

Did You Ever Disagree With A Decision Made At Work And Why?

How Would Your Colleagues And Boss Describe You?

Why The Gap In Your Employment?

What Are The Reasons Why You Changed Career Paths?

How Do You Handle Pressure And Situations That Are Stressful?

Tell Me About Your Salary Requirements?

What Do You Do When You Are Not Working?

Questions You Should Ask The Interviewer

The Interview Is Actually A Two-Way Street, While Your Potential Employer Is Asking Several Questions To Know More About You And Your Skills; You Also Need To Respond With Valid Questions. Therefore, You Have To Prepare Questions Relating To The Company, The Position And Your Boss Just To Be Sure That It Is The Right Position For You. The Hiring Manager Will Get The Impression That You Are Not Interested In The Job Or You Did Not Prepare Well If You Do Not Have Questions.

The Chance To Ask Questions Often Comes At The End Of The Interview So Have At Least Two Excellent Questions To Demonstrate Your Interest And Indicate That You Have Researched The Company. So, Consider The Following Examples Of Questions You Should Ask In An Interview:

In Your Opinion, What Are The Most Crucial Qualities Someone Needs To Excel In This Role? You Will Get Valuable Information That May Not Be In The Job Description When You Ask This Question. In Addition, You Will Know More About The Culture And Expectations Of The Company, Which Will Help You, Prove That You Are Qualified For The Job.

What Are The Daily Responsibilities Of This Job? You Will Learn More About The Role By Asking This Question So You Can Decide Whether The Job Is Right For You. You Will Also Gain More Insights Into Skills And Strengths That The Company Needs.

Who Do You Think Is Your Top Competitor And Why? Although You Should Have Known About Their Competitor From Your

Research, You Will Get More Information, Which You May Not Find Elsewhere.

What Is The Next Phase Of The Interview Process? This Question Indicates That You Are Ready To Move Forward In The Process And It Will Help You Obtain Vital Information Regarding The Timeline For Hiring To Enable You To Follow Up Appropriately.

When Asking Questions, Avoid Asking About Benefits Or Salaries Until You Get To The Final Steps In The Interview Process.

Dealing With Illegal And Inappropriate Interview Questions

During An Interview, Specific Questions Should Be Off-Limits. These Include Questions About Citizenship, Ancestry, Credit Rating, Age, Disabilities, Criminal Record, Military Discharge, Family Status, Gender Or Your Religion. Although The Purpose Of Such Questions May Be To Ascertain Whether You Are Qualified For The Job Or Not, The Questions Should Not Be Asked Directly By Your Interviewer.

These Questions Are Lawful If The Hiring Manager Can Prove That They Are Bona Fide Occupational Qualifications That Are Reasonably Essential To The Normal Operation Of The Business. So, What Happens When Asked Such Questions? When You Face Illegal Questions In An Interview Or The Questions Start To Follow An Unlawful Trend, You Have The Option Of Refusing To Answer Or Even End The Interview. You May Be Better Off Discovering Whether The Questions You Are Being Asked In An Interview Are An Indication Of The Company Policies.

In Some Cases, The Hiring Manager May Mistakenly Ask Inappropriate Questions, So You Can Choose, In That Instance, To Politely Answer By Avoiding The Substance Of The Question While Dealing With The Intent. In Case You Feel That You Have Been A Victim Of Discrimination By An Employer, Employment Agency Or Labor Union When Applying For A Position Or During A Job Due To Race, Sex, Nationality, Disability Or Other Factors, You May File A Charge Of Discrimination.

How To Answer Behavior-Based Interviews
Behavior-Based Interviews Are Designed To Determine How Well You Will Perform On The Job. The Fundamental Principle Behind This Method Is That The Perfect Indicator Of The Future Behavior Of An Individual Is The Past Behavior. The Traditional Interview Will Go Through The Applicant's Resume With Open-Ended Questions.

On The Other Hand, Behavioral Interview Will Include Several Standardized Questions That Are Designed To Compel You To Discuss How You Responded Or Handled Certain Situations Before. Each Response Is Expected To Describe Some Situations About Your Past And The Observations And Feelings You Have About Them. So, What Are The Possible Behavior-Based Interview Questions You Should Expect?

Describe A Complicated Issue You Tried Resolving? How Were You Able To Identify The Problem? How Did You Attempt Solving The Problem? (This Questioned Is

Aimed At Making You Demonstrate Problem-Solving Skill)

Tell Me About A Time You Tried Persuading A Colleague Or A Friend To Do Something They Initially Were Not Willing To Do (This Shows Leadership)

Talk About A Time You Made A Personal Decision To Get Something Done, And You Finished The Task. (This Demonstrates Initiative).

When Answering Behavior-Based Interview Questions, You Must Be Familiar With The Job You Are Being Interviewed For. Visit The Job Description And Find Out More About The Job. You Must Learn To Draw From Several Experiences, Which Will Demonstrate Your Abilities And Skills. You Can Provide A Great Story By Combining Work Experience And Non-Work Experience. Also, Take Advantage Of Quotes From Your Bosses Or Customers When Answering The Questions.

Using The "Situation Or Task, Action, And Result" (Star) Approach Can Give Structure And Focus To Your Answers. Also, Make Use Of Recent Examples Because You Will

Undoubtedly Be Asked For Details Regarding The Situation. You May Forget Some Details Of Situations That Have Exceeded 18 Months. However, Using Fresh Examples Will Provide You With Information That Is More Explicit. Practice Answering Some Of The Behavior-Based Questions By Learning To Tell Stories Until You Are Capable Of Delivering Vivid And Concise Stories That Will Not Exceed Three Minutes.

Sending A Thank-You Note

Sending A Thank You Note Offers You Several Benefits; It Helps You Remind Your Prospective Employer Of The Skills And Abilities You Offer When Hired. Sending An Email Affords You The Chance To Include Your Online Portfolio As Well As Professional Social Networking Profiles. Sending A Thank You Note Is A Way To Appreciate Your Interviewer For The Opportunity To Meet With Them. There Are Several Ways To Send A Thank You Note; It Can Be An Email, A Phone Call Or A Written Note. Since Most Things Are Now Done Digitally, Sending An Email Will

Be One Of The Most Preferred Ways Of Sending A Thank You Note.

Endeavor To Keep Your Email Free From Grammatical Errors Or Wrong Spelling. Avoid Sending A Message That Is Too Casual; There Should Be No Memes Or Internet Acronyms. Your Email Should Not Exceed A Thank You Email And Subsequent Follow-Up In A Week. If You Continue Sending More Emails, You Will End Up Promoting Yourself And Stress The Interviewer Out. When Sending The Email, Make Sure You Send It With 24 Hours Of The Interview. Ensure You Include All Your Interviewers In The Email And Let The Name Of The Position Should Be In The Subject Line As Well As The Words "Thank You."

You Also Need To Remind The Hiring Manager Of Your Qualifications By Mentioning The Keywords In The Original Job Listing. If You Have Links To Your Portfolio Or Other Professional Sites, Try To Include Them.

Chapter 11: The Right Look

Appropriate Dress

Just As You Wouldn't Wear A Bathing Suit To A Cocktail Party, The Clothes You Wear To An Interview Are Important. Yes, We've Heard It All Before. You're An Individual, A Nonconformist. People Shouldn't Be Judged By Their Clothes, But Their Talent. And On And On It Goes. The Reality Is, Right Or Wrong People Are Judged By What They Wear.

It Wouldn't Make Sense For A Fashion Designer To Hire A Person Who Came To An Interview In Muddy Jeans And A Ketchup Stained T-Shirt. Just Like A Farmer Would Raise His Brows If A Hired Hand Arrived In A Three-Piece Suit To Bail Hay. No Matter How Much The Potential Employee Claims To Know Or How Wonderful Their Portfolio Is, Their Outer Appearance Would Undermine Their Interview Performance And Skill Set.

Clothes Tell An Employer You Understand What Is Expected Of You. They Also Tell

Him Or Her A Lot About Who You Are. This Has Nothing To Do With Labels Or How Expensive The Clothing Is. It Has Everything To Do With Social Cues, Appropriateness And The Ability To Fit In And Be A Team Player. Your Uniform Whether It's An Actual Uniform Or The Unspoken Uniform Of The Office, Tells Those You Work With That You Belong To Their Group, And Sets The Tone That You Are Ready And Willing To Work.

Many Offices Have Adapted A Relaxed Dress Code, But Unless You Know That For A Fact Before An Interview, Don't Show Up In Cut Offs And Your Favorite University Sweatshirt. You Don't Have To Wear A Suit And Tie Or Dress (Unless The Office Requires It). But Dress Pants Or Khakis, Button Down Shirts Or Polos, Clean Shoes (Something Beside Athletic Shoes) Demonstrate That You Are A Professional, Who At The Very Least Cleans Up Nicely For This One Day. It Shows Respect For The Importance Of The Job, Your Employer, And The Position. It Says, You

Will Take Your Work Seriously And Can Be An Asset To The Organization.

Body Language

Whole Books Have Been Written On Business Body Language. In Fact, It's So Important That Body Language Experts Are Often Hired In High Profile Court Cases To Help Select A Jury And Read Their Language During A Trial. While Beyond The Scope Of This Book, Here Are A Few Key Points.

Arrival

Make Sure You Appear Confident From The Minute You Walk In To A Professional Interview. Some Employers Like To Watch Potential Employees From A Hidden Location Before They Introduce Themselves. Use Good Posture, Hold Your Head Up, And Speak With Confidence Even When Speaking To The Receptionist.

Very Often The Person At The Front Desk Will Take Your Name And Ask You To Have A Seat. Graciously Thank Him And Move Off A Few Steps But Remain Standing. Remaining Standing Tells Those Around

You That You Are A Busy Individual Who Values Time And Shouldn't Be Kept Waiting. It Also Conveys Confidence. While It Often Makes The Receptionist Nervous, It Also Makes You Difficult To Ignore. If You Are Left Waiting Too Long, They Will Likely Call Back To The Interviewer To Hurry Them Along, Without You Saying A Word.

While You Are Waiting, Prepare For The Interview. If It Is Winter, Take Off Your Coat. Either Find A Place To Hang It, Or Neatly Fold It, And Drape It Over Your Left Arm. That Way You Won't Have To Fumble With It When It Is Time To Shake Hands With Your Right Hand And Go Into Your Interview.

If You Must Carry An Accessory Such As A Back Pack, Brief Case, Portfolio, Or Purse, Carry Only One Extra Thing. The More Things You Have, The More Difficult It Is To Maneuver Through Tight Halls And Cramped Office Spaces. You Want To Appear Organized And Ready To Work Or Display Your Skills—Not Fumble With Additional Baggage. Women Who Carry

Purses Might Opt Instead To Carry A Portfolio, Keep Their Purse In The Car Under The Seat, And Put Their Keys In A Pocket. Anything To Downsize And Lessen The Clutter.

Carrying Only One Additional Item Also Helps When It Comes To That Handshake. Items Won't Have To Shifted Or Set Down To Make Contact.

Handshakes

A Firm, Not Too Tight Handshake Is Always Best. And Interviewee Should Approach The Handshake As Equals. In Other Words, Extend Your Hand From The Side To Meet An Interviewer's Hand, As Opposed To From Above Or Below. Shaking A Hand With Your Hand On Top, Sends An Inappropriate Message Of Dominance. Whereas Shaking You Hand From Below Would Silently Send A Message Of Meagerness. Likewise Grasping Their Hand In Both Of Yours, Sends The Inappropriate Message Of Intimacy Or Being A Little Too Friendly.

Seating

When Sitting, Men In Particular, Need To Be Mindful Of Spreading Out Too Far. This Can Be Seen On Buses Or The Subway When Men Sit With Their Legs Spread Far Apart, Arms Extended Full Length Across The Back Of The Seats, Possibly Taking Up Additional Space For Coats Or Packages. On Mass Transit, It Sends The Message To Stay Away (Which Might Be A Plus In Certain Situations). In The Office A Variation Of Wide Spread Legs While Seated Can Be Interpreted As Overly Comfortable, Cocky, Sloppy, Or An Inappropriate Attempt To Exert Dominance.

It Is Best For Either Gender To Sit Up Straight. Legs Should Either Be Flat On The Floor, One Foot Tucked Slightly Behind The Other, Or Crossed. Hands Should Be Comfortable. Folding Them In Your Lap Or Keeping Them Loosely At Your Sides Is Always Acceptable. If You're An Animated Speaker, Don't Be Afraid To Use Your Hands, But It Might Be A Good Idea To Reel It In And Keep Gestures To A

Minimum Or More Conservative Than Usual.

When In Doubt At An Interview, Err On The Side Of Conservativism. This Has Nothing To Do With Politics. With Dress, Gestures, Opinions It's Easier To Expand On Them Later Than To Try To Retract Them After The Fact.

In Most U.S. Business Settings, It's Considered Good Manners To Look Directly Into The Eyes Of Your Interviewer. However, In Some Other Cultures This Is Seen As A Challenge Or Sign Of Disrespect. Therefore, It's Important If Interviewing For A Job In Another Country To Research Local Culture And Customs Ahead Of Time.

If Offered A Choice, Choose A Chair Directly Across From Your Interviewer. It's The Best Way To Keep Eye Contact. It Also Puts The Interviewee And Interviewer On Equal Footing. Standing Over Someone Or Sitting In A Higher Chair Or At A Higher Angle Exerts Dominance. Sitting To The Side, Forces Others To Turn To Look At Us. Neither Of These Scenarios Is Preferable In An Interview Situation.

If You Sit On The Far Side Of A Desk From Your Interviewer, Ask Before Placing Your Hands Or Your Things On Their Desk. Doing So Without Asking Can Be Seen As Arrogant, Overly Confident, Assumptive, Or Pushy.

Attention

Interviewees Demonstrate Attentiveness By Sitting Forward In Their Seat Or Leaning Slightly Forward So That Their Body Angles Toward The Interviewer. An Interviewee Might Also Tilt Their Head Toward The Interviewer. Of Course Smiling Often Conveys Interest, As Does Nodding.

If An Interviewer Begins To Fidget, Look Away, Check Their Phone, Or Seems Distracted, Chances Are They've Lost Interest In What The Interviewee Is Saying. It's A Nonverbal Cue To Move On.

An Interviewer That Places A Hand On Their Chin Or Props Their Head In Hand Or Over Their Mouth, Is Likely To Be Less Interested In What An Interviewee Is Saying. Propping A Hand On The Face Is Usually A Way Of Trying To Stay Focused When One Has Lost Interest. Putting A

Hand Over One's Mouth Could Be A Way To Stifle Yawns. However, It Could Also Be A Way To Subconsciously Stop From Saying Something They Would Rather Not Say. This Could Be As Simple As Suppressing An Opinion Or As Serious As Covering A Lie.

Mirroring

Mirroring Is The Ability To Reflect Another Person's Body Language In Your Own. For Example, If A Person Clasps Their Hands Behind Their Back While Speaking To You, You Might Mirror Their Body Language By Doing Something Similar. A Prime Example Of Mirrored Body Language Can Be Seen By Watching Vice President Pence When He's With President Trump. Quite Frequently, You Might See The President Take A Drink Of Water, Only To Be Mirrored A Few Seconds Later By The Vice President.

Mirroring Is Often Done Subconsciously. It Can Be Used To Express Unity Or Connectivity. But It Can Also Be Used To Reflect A Comfortable Or Subservient Position. If You're Not Sure What To Do Or

How To Act During The Interview Process, Adopt A Similar Stance To Your Interviewer.

The Whole Sentence

Reading Body Language Is Intuitive, But It's Also Unique To Ever Situation. The Main Thing To Remember Is That Movements And Gestures Shouldn't Be Read In Isolation. It's Important To Take In The Context Of The Setting, Extenuating Circumstances, And The Rest Of The Body Sentence.

For Example, If An Interviewer Shivers It Might Mean That She Dislikes What An Interviewee Says, But She Might Also Be Cold. If The Interviewer Also Has A Pink Nose And Rubs Her Arms, Body Sentence Tells The Interviewee She's Cold. But If She Shakes Her Head, Raises Her Brows, Or Looks Away, She's Likely Conveying A Less Favorable Opinion.

As An Interviewee, Be Ready To Read The Whole-Body Sentence Of Your Interviewer To Help Determine What You Say And How You Say It.

Chapter 12: Capabilities & Facing Challenges

Also They Test Whether You Can Work Under Pressure. They Will Check How Efficient You Are In Winning And Convincing Superiors And Colleges. Here I Jot Down Some Typical Questions That They May Ask You. You Have To Answer Very Sensibly To All These Questions. It's A Simple Test To Know Whether You Could Handle Multi Tasks. By The Answers You Give, They Judge You Whether You Have The Potential To Tackle The Job And Get An Idea Of Your Team Spirit And People Convincing Ability.

In The Year 1998, The Minor Employees Struck Work Suddenly On A Labor Issue At The Tail End Of Manufacturing Process. The Machine Operator Is Absent, You Have Plenty Of Partly Turned Out Units To Be Passed Through Machine For Final Finishing And You Are Supposed To Prepare The Products For Tomorrow's

Shipment. How Do You Tackle The Situation?

You Are A Team Leader Of One Of The Work Teams In Your Department, Team Leader Of Another Team In Your Department Suddenly Fall Sick. No Other Suitable Person Is Available To Lead That Team. In Such A Situation Can You Over Look His Responsibilities While Leading Your Team?

Have You Ever Acted In A Higher Position For More Than Six Months In Any Of The Companies You Worked In The Past? Have You Shown Any Improvements In Work During The Period? If Yes Can You Brief About The Acting Period?

Can You Tell Us Of Any Unforgettable Experience Of Yours, During Your Career?

When Answering Above Questions You Are Supposed To Use Your Experiences, Job Knowledge And Professionalism. You Have To Always Give Quite Positive Answers Explaining How You Would Deal With Such Situations. Applying With Your Common Sense Also Will Push You Forward. As The Above Questions Can Be

Considered As Tough Questions That Will Be Raised To Candidates I Can Help You By Providing Some Positive Answers To Them.

I Will Negotiate With Other Line Managers And Team Leaders And Hire A Machine Operator From Another Section; I Myself Personally Assist Him To Operations Because The Stuff Has To Be Prepared For Tomorrow's Shipment.

Yes, Most Certainly. Production Is Most Important. I Am Duty Conscious And Try To Give My Best Performances To Company.

Yes. Please Refer To My Resume Under Employment History & Special Achievements. I Have Acted For Site Engineer For Eight Months, After Successful Acting Period I Was Rewarded With The Positive Alternatives Other Than Completing Manufacture Process Without Wasting The Raw Materials Of A High Cost.

I Could Convince The Middle Management, Supervisory Categories To Complete The Full Process.

Final Interview

Now Candidates Have Passed Preliminary, First Interviews And Were Selected For The Final Interview. Management Will Consider Calling Only The Very Best Candidates To Final Interview, After Being Strained For Several Occasions According To Merits Of First Two Interviews. I Must Mention Here, That Some Superiors Are Not In Favor Of Conducting More Than One Interview As Per Their Time Management. Whatever Hr Manager Advises They Will Not Listen And They Themselves Do Final Selections Only After Reference Checking And Solely Depending On Somebody's Recommendation. Ultimately A Person Not Suitable To Operate In The Vacant Position Will Be Absorbed And It Will Be A Complete Loss To Company. This Type Of Interviews Doesn't Analyze The Real Meaning Of The Word "Inter – View"

We Have Discussed About Stages Of Interviews, Preparation For Interview, Interview Competency, Interview Techniques & Other Important Factors In Length. I Have Provided Guidance And

Important Hints To Face Interviews Successfully. Hope You Have Grasped All The Information Correctly. Final Interview Will Be The Last Stage And Only One Person Will Succeed. Interview Board Has All Information Of Finally Selected People And They Will Submit Their Report To The Chairman, Managing Director Or Ceo To View The Report Before Commencement Of Final Interview. Most Probably The Chief Administrator Of The Company Also Will Participate In Final Interview.

Some Times They May Have To Select The Most Suitable Person Out Of Two Or Three. Prior To Final Interview It's The Responsibility Of The Hr Manager To Do Reference Checking Of The Candidates. Interview Panel Will Sit For The Interview With All Information Of Employees Including Reference Check Report. This Will Be A Very Friendly Type Of Interview As All Tough Questions Have Been Raised To Them In Early Interviews. They Will Probably Ask Some General & Professional Questions. Here Are Some Typical Questions To Guide You.

Q: Have You Informed Your Superiors About The Progress Of Your Interview? Can You Report Within A Month Or How Long It Will Take To Get Released From Present Place?

A: I Have Informed Them Of My Interview, As Per The Terms In My Letter Of Appointment I Have To Give One Calendar Months Notice In Advance. They Got To Find A Suitable Replacement Too. If I Am Selected, There Are Some Procedures To Follow To Get Released. Anyway I Am In Good Books With Them I Can Negotiate Favorably.

Q: In Case If You Are Selected, Would You Like To Work To This Salary + Other Packages? This Is The Salary Structure For This Position; Leaving Starting Point And First Stage Of The Structure If You Place You On Second Stage Is You Ok? (They Produce Salary Structure For You To Go Through)

A: Sir, I Am Unable To Get An Idea Immediately. I Have Some Things To Know About, Can I Ask Some Thing?

Q: Yes Most Certainly, What Are Those?

A: (Your Verifications Must Be Situational Based. So I Leave It To You To Decide)

Interview Boards' Verification: They May Explain Things Very Clearly For You To Understand.

Q: Any Thing Else You Want To Know?

A: No Sir.

Interview Board: Ok Thank You So Much For Attending Interview, We Will Let You Know The Result.

Please Do Not Forget To Thank All The Members Of Interview Board In Return By Shaking Hands.

Now In Final Interview Candidates Are Free To Ask Any Questions, Relevant To Job Position, Wages Etc. Interview Board Is Bound To Explain Clearly To Their Questions.

Chapter 13: The Swot Analysis

One Of The Most Useful Tools You Can Employ To Aid In The Planning Process Is The Swot Analysis. For Anyone Unfamiliar With This Tool, Swot Stands For Strengths, Weaknesses, Opportunities, And Threats. The Swot Analysis Is Among The Most Widely Used Business Analytics Tools, Particularly Among Those Engaged In Strategic Planning. Whether It's A Young Company Just Getting Off The Ground, A Mature Business Conducting A Five-Year Strategic Plan, Or Business Executives Assessing The Viability Of An Investment, The Swot Analysis Is Used To Provide A Detailed Snapshot Of The Internal And External Environmental Factors That Impact Success Or Failure. Put More Simply, The Swot Analysis Is An Examination Of The Environmental Factors That Affect One's Ability To Achieve A Certain Objective. So What Does This Have To Do With You?

As It Relates To Your Goal Of Finding A Job, It Is A Tool To Provide You With A Realistic Depiction Of Where You Stand Relative To Your Objective. Here Is A Simple Overview: **Strengths** And **Weaknesses** Are Considered **Internal Factors**, Meaning Largely Within Your Own Personal Control. **Opportunities** And **Threats** Are Considered **External Factors,** Meaning Largely Outside Of Your Control.

Internal Environment: Your Internal Environment Consists Of All The Factors Within Your Individual Or Organizational Control.

Examples:

Strengths: Education, Language Proficiency, Technical Proficiency, Management Experience, Security Clearance, Strong Network. In Other Words, What Do You Bring To The Table That Improves Your Chances Of Achieving Your Goal?

Weaknesses: Lack Of Education Or Experience, Expired Professional License Or No License/Certification, No Security Clearance. In Other Words, What Are Your

Personal/Professional Deficiencies Or Liabilities That Inhibit Your Ability To Attain Your Goal?

<u>External Environment</u>: Your External Environment Consists Of Forces Beyond Your Control.

Examples:

Opportunities: Intra-Organizational Career Opportunities, Access To Education, Or Governmental Push Toward Hiring Minorities, Veterans, Or Women. In Other Words, What Are The Current Or Future Conditions That Can Play A Role In Helping You Achieve Your Goal?

Threats: Economic, Market, And Demographic Trends, Legislation. In Other Words, What Current Or Future Forces Or Conditions Beyond Your Control That Can Hinder Your Ability To Achieve Your Goal?

Employing The Swot Analysis Will Help You Evaluate Your Capabilities Against The Requirements Of The Objective, Which, For Most Of You, Means Landing The Right Job. Once You Have Examined All Of The Factors That Comprise The Swot Analysis, You Will Be Able To Better Identify Ways

You May Exploit Your Strengths And Opportunities, Or Else Mitigate Your Weaknesses And Threats. The Swot Analysis Is A Useful Tool In That It Forces You To Give Serious Thought To The Factors Or Conditions Affecting Your Internal And External Environment, Factors You May Not Otherwise Have Considered.

Although Not A Requirement, Many Planners Often Create A Graphical Depiction Of The Swot To Illustrate The Results. The Most Important Thing, However, Is To Get The Information On Paper. It Is The **Information** Itself That Is Most Important, Not The Way It Is Represented. The Matrix Depiction Typically Associated With The Swot Analysis Is Merely An Example Of How You Can Display Or Convey The Information.

A Major Benefit Of The Swot Analysis, In Addition To Informing Your Planning And Decision-Making Efforts, Is That It Can Aid You In Developing The Questions Used During The Informational Interview. What I Mean Is That When You Interview

People, Your Aim Will Be To Ask Targeted, Strategic Questions That Are Intended To Elicit The Types Of Answers That Help Move You Closer To Your Goal. The Types Of Questions You Ask The Interviewee Will Be Largely A Reflection Of The Information You Uncovered During Your Swot Analysis, Particularly With Respect To Overcoming Any Challenges You May Face. It Is Also A Great Way To Organize All The Factors That Can Help Or Hurt Your Ability To Attain Your Goal(S). Here Is An Example Of How It Might Work. Let's Say That You Are Interested In A Particular Career Path And You Want To Analyze Your Ability To Pursue That Career. Let's Say Further That You Are Interested In Becoming A Sports Agent. The First Thing You Will Want To Do Is Research The Necessary Qualifications For Pursuing This Career Field. Once You Have Identified The Criteria, You Will Need To Measure Your Qualifications, Strengths And Weaknesses Against The Qualifications Of The Sports Agent Career Field. Once You Have Completed Your Swot Analysis, You Should

Have A Solid Understanding Of What You Bring To The Table Along With Areas You May Need To Improve Upon To Achieve Your Goal.

	Positive	Negative
Internal	**S** List all of your strengths, assets, and qualifications that can help you become a sports agent. This may also include your personal and professional network. List everything you can think of.	**W** List any personal and professional liabilities that can hinder your ability to become a sports agent. May include a lack of professional qualifications, lack of education, or an absence of necessary personal qualities.
External	**O** List any conditions that may present opportunities for you to explore (e.g. expanding your professional network). Successful agent make their living off of developing relationships.	**T** List any obstacles outside of your control that can either make it more difficult or even prevent you from becoming an agent.

Chapter 14: The Phone Interview!

"I'm A Great Believer In Luck, And I Find The Harder I Work, The More I Have Of It."— —Thomas Jefferson

The Phone Interview Is Seen As The Primer For The Main In-Person Interview. It Often Sets The Tone For What You Should Expect Next. The Phone Interview Is Often Used To Get A Handle On The Candidates Vying For Any Particular Position And Narrowing The Prospective Pool Of Applicants.

It Is Usually Conducted By A Single Individual But Sometimes Could Be Done By A Group Or Panel. The Phone Interview Will Usually Come After Certain Resume Criteria Have Been Met. It Could Also Follow A Psychometric Test Portion Of The Recruitment Process. Phone Interviews Are Favorites For Recruitment Firms, Then Sales And Marketing Firms; Although You Can't Exclude Other Firms From Using Them Especially When Location Is A Challenge. According To Recent Studies,

Phone Interviews Typically Last Around 36 Minutes On The Average.

Why A Phone Interview?

For The Interviewer The Pluses Of Conducting The Phone Interview Are Mainly:

Savings In Cost Of Conducting The Interview:

Before The Popularity Of Phone Interviews Rose, A Lot Of Employers Were Condemned To Paying Huge Fees For Bringing In Candidates From Far And Wide Across The Country. As You Can Imagine This Practice Wasn't Very Cost Effective Especially When Compared To The Return On Investment.

Time Saving:

Time Has Always Been And Remains One Of The Most Valuable Resources Either An Applicant Or An Employer Will Ever Have. No One Wants To Spend Hours On A Flight And More Hours In A Hotel Room All For The Sake Of A Job Position They Might Not Even Be A Good Fit For. For The Employer There Is No Pint Tying Up Some Of Your Best Man Power Down For Days On End In

A Sometimes Pointless Exercise Of Trying To Find The Right Fit For A Job. Not To Mention The Vast Funds Wasted On Funding The Flights Of Various Candidates From Around The Country. Why Not Narrow The Pool Down A Great Deal Till Your Odds Are Much Higher That You Have Actually Found "The One"? The Simple Solution Is The Phone Interview.

Despite Having Advantages, Like Everything Else In Life, There Are Disadvantages To Phone Interviews On Both Sides. For The Interviewee The Major Disadvantages Are:

It's Impossible To See The Interviewer To Determine Their Responses To Certain Answers And Make And Subsequently Make Adjustments (This Doesn't Count If It's A Video Call Though, More About That Later).

The Phone Interview Times Might Sometimes Be Unexpected. The Time You Might Get A Call For The Interview Might Not Be The Most Convenient Time But For Fear Of Not Getting A Second Chance,

Most Applicants Entertain The Call Anyway.

Since You Really Don't Know The Exact Times Of The Interview, Nerves Might Play A Big Role In How Well You Perform.

Phone Interviews Are Usually More Formal, Intense And Often Contain A High Number Of Questions At A Frenetic Pace. There Is Usually Little Time To Think Of Answers To Questions.

Tips For Acing The Phone Interview

Have Your Phone Always:

Be Prepared. There Can Be Nothing More Irritating To An Interviewer Than Making The Call To A Potential Employee And Having To Deal With "Who Is This? ", "Huh" Or " Hang On A Moment." After All, These People Are Human Like You And I And After Making Thirty Calls In A Day It Can Get Quite Tiresome. Don't Get Your Interview Off On The Wrong Foot. Have The Interviewer Call Your Personal Cell Phone Number And Always Have It Around. If You're Using A House Phone Let Everyone Around Be Aware Of The

Interview And Be Prepared To Help You Take The Call.

Take The Call In A Quiet Room:

As Much As We Might Like To Be Prepared For The Phone Interview, Sometimes It Still Manages To Catch Us Unawares. If The Interview Call Catches You Unawares You Should Politely Request A Minute To Go Somewhere Secluded. Having Your Interview In The Quiet Comfort Of A Secluded Area Will Help Your Performance And Ease Nerves On Both Ends. Imagine Trying To Hear, Answer And Carry Out A Productive Conversation On A Public Transit Bus. The Chances You'll Make Much Headway At Putting Up An Impressive Performance Are Certainly Slimmer.

Check Your Voice Messages:

Are You One Of Those Who Have Annoying Answering Messages That Even Your Mum Thinks Is A Pain? Then You'd Better Not Forget To Change That To Something You'll Be Proud To Have Your Prospective Employer Hear. You Never Know When Your Prospective Employer Might Try To

Reach Out To You Concerning Your Job Application. It Might Just Be That Unprofessional Message That Makes The Caller Decide You Are Not Such A Good Fit For The Organization After All. I'm Sure You Agree That Would Be A Huge Price To Pay For Being A Little Bit "Unprofessional".

Keep Up With Your Documentation:

One Certainty With Any Kind Of Interview Is That You'll Be Asked Questions And Interviewed Based On The Content Of Your Resume. It Would Shock You To Know How Many Applicants Don't Remember The Details Of Positions Held And Duties Done Written On Their Resumes. These Gaps In Knowledge Only Make The Candidate Seem Incompetent, And Possibly A Liar. It Would Be Useful To Always Have Copies Of The Application For That Particular Position, Job Description And Copy Of The Original Ad, Cover Letter, As Well As Your Resume Handy Before And During Any Phone Interview.

Know Your Strengths:

I Know That Seems Like Quite An Obvious Statement But There's Much More To It Than It Seems. How Many Times Have You Actually Sat Down To Evaluate What You Do Best? It Is Something That Needs To Be Done With Every Single Job Application. You Need To Take A Look At The Job Description, Examine It Down To The Minutest Details, And Work Out What Unique Strengths You Bring To The Job. Interviewing Is All About Selling Yourself To Your Employer. It's All About Your Employer Knowing Why You Should Be Picked Ahead Of The Thousand Or So Other Applicants Vying For That Same Position. Every Good Sales Person Knows A Great Product Always Has Its (Usp) Unique Selling Points.

Be Enthusiastic:

Even If You Can't Be Seen During A Phone Interview It's Vital To Be Enthusiastic As Your Demeanor Easily Carries Through Over The Phone. A Phone Interview Is No Excuse To Slouch In Your Couch Or Lie In Bed To Take The Interview. You'll Not Be Doing Yourself Any Favors By Taking Either

Of These Actions. Slouching Or Lying In Bed Will Immediately Make You Come Off As Uninterested Or Bored. Hiring Managers Or Interviewers Always Look For Enthusiasm. If You're Perceived As Unenthusiastic During The Interview It Quickly Registers In The Interviewer's Mind That You Are Not A Good Fit For The Job. Smile While You're Talking, Not Too Much Of A Smile, But A Slight One. It Can Dramatically Improve The Image You Project Over The Phone. Also You Might Want To Sit Upright Or Stand At A Desk For The Duration Of The Call. It Portrays You As Alert And Interested.

Speak Clearly:

It Certainly Won't Help If Whoever You're On A Phone Interview With Doesn't Understand You Clearly. With The Diverse Cultural Backgrounds Within The Global Workforce Of Employers, Hiring Managers, And Recruiting Specialists From All Over The World, It Would Be Smart To Communicate In The Safest Way Possible. Your Safest Bet To Being Heard And Understood Clearly Is To Speak Slowly And

Clearly. Don't Speak Too Slowly But Not Too Quickly As Well. It's A Fine Line, But It Helps If You Make A Conscious Effort To Be Understood And Establish Clear Lines Of Communication. Also, Indirectly Repeating And Reaffirming What The Interviewer Has Said Will Build A Clear Connection Between Both Parties. You Might Say "I've Heard What You Said About Probably Having To Work Long Hours And I'm No Stranger To That. I Worked Long Hours At My Previous Job Even When I Wasn't Required To, But I Did It Just Because My Work Was So Interesting. "

Video Interviews

A Few Words Are Necessary On The Subject Of Video Interviews Which Are Becoming Increasingly Commonplace As A Means Of Recruiting Promising Prospects Into Organizations. Like Phone Interviews, Video Interviews Help The Employer Or Recruiting Agency Save Money On The Logistics Of Flying Candidates To The Location Of An Interview Especially If The Best And Most Qualified Candidates Do Not Reside In Or Around The Location.

The Rules To Follow When Handing Video Interviews Are Not Different From What Should Be Followed When On A Phone Interview. The Only Difference Between Both Interview Types Is That Your Features Are Visible To The Interviewer Or Recruiter.

Some Important Tips To Follow When Handling The Video Interview Are To Set Up All Your Equipment And Make Sure Everything Works The Way It Should. Interviewers Will Only Request A Video Interview If It's Necessary, So You Want To Ensure You Can Be Seen. Be Sure To Get On To The Video Call At Least 20 Minutes Before The Actual Meeting Time; You'll Need To Be Able To Sort Out Any Technical Hitches You Might Have On Your End.

Make Sure The Room Is Well Lit And Do Not Set Your Computer Directly In Front Of A Strong Light Source Like A Window Or Lamp As That Would Produce A Lot Of Glare On Your Features For The Person Viewing You On The Other End. You Want Your Features To Be As Clear As Possible Without Being Too Bright.

Don't Forget To Clear Up The Room Of Anything That Might Not Be Necessary. Clutter Around The Room Is A No-No, Your Resume Would Most Likely Say You're Organized And Good With Details; That Should Be Reflected In The Way Your Room Looks.

Chapter 15: Put Forth Confidence In The Interview

Even The Most Self-Assured Candidate Is Nervous During A Job Interview; However, You Should Portray An Image Of Confidence.

Always Make Eye Contact- Nothing Is More Of A Dead Give Away Of Poor Self-Confidence Than A Person That Will Not Look Someone In The Eye. Walk Up To Your Interviewer, Extend Your Hand And Look In Them In The Eye When You Greet Them And Express Your Pleasure Of Meeting Them. Keep In Mind That You Got The Interview In The First Place Because You Were Qualified, So Use This Knowledge To Build And Strengthen Your Confidence. Your Confidence Level Will Build Over Time As You Attend More Interviews.

Be Truthful In The Interview

Always Tell The Truth And Never Lie In An Interview To Make Yourself Sound Better Then You Actually Are. Do Not Tell

Anything That Cannot Be Verified By Your Current Or Former Boss Or The References That You Provide. Not Being Honest With Your Education Is A Good Way To Get Into Trouble, So If Don't Have A Degree Don't Proclaim To Have One. Play Up The Positive Attributes; If You Were Part Of A Project Tell The Interviewer About The Part You Played And How You Contributed To The Overall Success Of The Project. Telling The Truth Will Always Put You In The Best Light.

Be Precise Answering Interview Questions
Although You Maybe Somewhat Nervous In A Job Interview, Try To Really Listen And Concentrate On The Question Before You Answer. If The Interviewer Tells You They Want A Specific Example, Don't Give A Generic Response Because This Is A Surefire Way Or Ruining Your Chance Of Getting The Job. These Types Of Questions Are Known As Situational Questions. If An Interviewer Were To Say To You, "Tell Us About Your Favorite Vacation City." You Wouldn't Respond By Telling Them About All The Cities You Would Like To Go Or

Make A Generalization: Potential Employers Are Trying To Determine How You React Or Perform In Specific Situations.

Common Questions That Are Asked Include:

"Tell Me About A Point In Time When You Led A Team Project." Include What The Project Was, How Many People, And Any Challenges That You Faced And How You Overcame Them.

"Tell Me About A Conflict You Had With A Co-Worker." Only Pick Situations That Had A Positive Outcome.

Employers Today Want To Know How You Are Going To Perform On The Job Before They Even Hire You. By Answering Situational Questions Specifically You Can Assure The Interviewer You Have The Skills And Thought Processes That They Are Looking For. Be Detailed But To The Point; You May Either Be A Person That Talks Furiously When They Are Nervous, Or One That Clam Up In A Stressful Situation – You Need To Be Conscious Of This And Not Do Either In An Interview. The Interview

Wants Enough Information That Will Help Them Understand What You Are Talking About, But Not Extraneous Irrelevant Information.

Try To Avoid Using Jargon Or Acronyms When Giving Examples From A Previous Or Current Job. Always Use Common Terms That The Vast Majority Of People Are Familiar With. When Speaking In Terms Of Projects, Tell What The Project Was About, How Many People And How Well You Managed The Project. The Interviewer Is Not Going To Be Interested In A Play By Play Of The Entire Project – They Want To Know Your Role In It. Try To Stay On Topic And Not To Get Sidetracked And Forget The Point You Were Trying To Make. It Is A Good Idea To Practice With A Friend Or Family Member Before Your Interview.

How To Answer The Hard Interview Questions

Each Interview Session Has At Least One Question That You Really Don't Know The Best Way To Answer. It Is The One That You Agonize Over For Days And Keep Going Over It And Over It In Your Head

And Ask Others How They Would Have Answered. There Is Not Way To Avoid These Types Of Questions But You Can Answer Them With Confidence To Give Yourself Peace Of Mind Until You Get A Call Back.

Do Not Feel That You Have To Answer Instantaneously After You Have Been Asked A Question. You Are Not On A Tv Game Show Where The Fastest Contestant To Answer Wins. Your Interviewers Will Appreciate That You Have Taken Time To Think And Formulate Your Answer. If You Are Concerned By A Prolonged Silence – Don't Be, It Is Normal. If You Have Been Asked A Question That You Do Not Know Exactly What To Say, Ask For A Moment To Think Of An Appropriate Answer. This Is Preferable To Taking A Long Time To Answer Without Explaining What You Are Doing.

If You Really Can't Think Of An Answer Promptly Ask If You Can Come Back To The Question In A Moment – Keep Trying To Think Of An Answer. Don't Think That If You Get To The End Of The Interview And

You Haven't Answered The Question That You Are Off Of The Hook. Even If Your Interviewer Doesn't Ask Again, It Has Not Gone Unnoticed That You Didn't Respond To A Question. The Best Case Scenario Is For You To Bring The Topic Back To The Question And Answer It Accordingly. Thank Your Interviewer For Giving You The Extra Time To Come Up With The Right Answer. If It Is A Lengthy Question That Is Broken Into Parts, Break It Down Into, Don't Try And Answer It All At Once – You Can Always Ask For Parts Of The Question To Be Repeated.

Pauses And Silences In The Interview

There Are Going To Be Times During An Interview When There Will Be Pauses In Conversation Or Complete Silence. This Can Be Initiated By You Or The Interviewer And In Most Cases Either Is Not An Indicator That Something Is Amiss. You Can Ask For A Moment To Think Of An Answer And During This Time There Is Most Likely Going To Be Complete Silence. This Is Fine And Perfectly Normal, Don't Get Distracted Because No One Is Talking,

Use The Time You Have Asked For Wisely And Think Of The Best Answer Or Example You Can Give. If The Interviewer Is Taking Notes (And Most Likely They Are), Be Comfortable With The Fact That There Is Going To Be Pauses In Between Questions As They Try And Write Everything Down. This Is Actually A Good Thing Because It Means They Have Liked What You Have To Say And Want To Remember It When They Are Later Making A Decision On Who To Hire.

If You Have Answered A Question And It Is Met By Silence And The Interviewer Is Not Writing Anything Done, You May Be At A Loss As To What You Should Do. It Could Signal That The Interview Is Expecting More Information Or They Are Not Satisfied With The Answer. You Won't Know Unless You Ask, "Do You Want Me To Elaborate On That?" If The Answer Is No, Just Patiently Wait For The Next Question To Be Asked. Don't Worry That The Interviewer Is Not Praising You On Your Answer To Each Question And Continue Onto The Next One. They Do

Not Want To Give You An Indication Of How You Are Doing During The Interview And Are Trained To Be Neutral When Responding To Answers, If They Respond At All.

Chapter 16: How To Search For A Job?

Making A Good Resume Is Still A Secondary Process When Put In Contrast To Look For Places To Send Your Resume. The Difference Between The Two Stages Is That The Process Of Resume Building Starts Very Early In Your Academic Life While Job Hunting Is A Much Farther Process, One That Doesn't Start Until Quite Later In One's University Life.

You Must Be Wondering About How People Know Where To Send Their Resumes. This Chapter Seeks To Make You Familiar With The Art Of Networking And Other Methods By Which You Can Ascertain As To What Places Deserve You.

Spread Your Web

It Is Vital That You Have A Good Network Amongst The Office Goers And The Corporate Middlemen. One Good Way To Do This Is By Regularly Interning At Places You Are Interested To Work At. It Is Necessary That You Have At Least A Dozen

Of Contacts That Either Work Or Are In Contact With Places Of Your Interest.

You May Have A Close Friend Or A Distant Cousin Working At A Place You Are Passionate To Work At. Get In Contact With Them And Ask About Possible Vacancies. Do Not Be Disheartened If There Are None But Do Remember To Stay In Touch. You Never Know When A Vacancy Comes Popping Up; When It Does You Should Be Just A Phone Call Away.

- Stay In Touch With Interns From Your Own Batch As Well As From Your Junior And Senior Batches. Do Not Be Reluctant To Ask For Help.
- Politely Ask For Job Recommendations From People Who Have Some Influence In The Corporate Circles. However, Be Suggestive In Your Tone And Not Assertive. Remember They Are Not Bound To Help You.
- Even If Someone Isn't Directly Useful To You Regarding Your Hunt For Jobs, Do Not Isolate Them From Your Personal Circle. You Never Know When Someone Who

Appears Useless Now Could Turn Into A Messiah The Next Day.

- Maintain A Diary Of Contacts That You Think Might Help You With Landing A Job Interview. Even A Mere Opportunity To Land An Interview Might Be Useful.

Be On The Look Out

A Job Won't Come To You Gift-Wrapped In The Courier Service. It Does Not Come As A Complimentary Gift Along With Your Pizza Order. It Is Not Something That You Are Born With Or You Acquire A Right To On The Basis Of Mere Citizenship. A Job Requires Tedious Efforts And Regular Trials. It's Called A 'Job-Hunt' For A Reason. You Need To Pursue Your Dream Job, Grab It When It Flies By And Never Let Go Of It.

For The Same, You Need To Be On Your Best Alert Mode Possible. Subscribe To Newspapers That Reserve A Separate Page For Job Vacancies And Advertisements. Such Corners In The Newspapers Are Called Classified.

Make It A Habit To Skim Through This Section Of Your Daily Newspaper At Least

Twice In A Day. Keep Your Contacts I Informed About Your Need To Land A Good Job. Distribute Your Phone Numbers Among These Contacts And Attend Your Calls Regularly.

The Internet Is A Gift- Use It!

Most Problems Of Today's World Are Solved At The Click Of A Mouse And A Few Click Clacks Of The Keyboard. The Internet Era Has Tried Its Best To Reduce Our Efforts. From Online Shopping To Payment Of Bills; Everything Has Been Made Possible With The Advent Of Internet.

When It Comes To Jobs, The Internet Hasn't Shied Away From Offering Help. There Are Many Sites That Display Job Vacancies Whenever They Are Available. There Are Sites That Offer You The Chance To Upload Your Resume And Offices And Workplaces Interested In You Will Contact You With The Help Of The Information Provided.

Internships

The Number Of People Landing Jobs Through Recruitment Is Almost As Equal To The Number Of People Landing Jobs

Through Internships. Internships Are The Work Periods A Non Employed Person Spends In A Workplace, Working Often Without Any Regular Payment. Internships Are Supposed To Achieve The Following Ends:

- Make The Internee Familiar With The Know-How Of The Work In An Office And Give Him An Understanding Of The Nature Of Work.
- Make Him Aware Of The Kind Of Work Environment In The Office He's Working At.
- Guide The Internee Regarding All The Detailed Knowledge A Prospective Employee Must Gain Before Joining The Workplace.

Internships Are A Great Way To Warm Up To A Workplace. You Not Only Stand A Chance Of Gaining Experience Working There, But Also Achieve An Edge Over Fresh Job Applicants. Having Worked With The Place, You Have The Chance To Boast Of Better Experiences Than The Rest And The Interviewers Will Surely Keep That In

Mind While Zeroing In On Their Final Choice.

To Sum It All Up, It Is Important That You Start Quite Early When It Comes To Spreading Your Network. A Good Network Works Wonders With Your Job Prospects.

Chapter 17: What To Do After The Interview

Now That Your Physical Interview Is Over, You Still Have A Need To Continue Forward With Making An Attention-Getting Great Impression On Your Interviewers And Potential Employer. Following Are Some Very Important "After Interview" Guidelines To Follow Which Will Serve To Enhance Your Presence Further, And Confirm Both Your Personal And Professional Ethics.

Important Steps To Follow After Your Interview Is Completed

1. Be Clear On Your Next Step - As Was Indicated In The Previous Section, Do Not Leave The Interview Room Without Having A Clear Understanding Of What The Next Step Of The Interviewing Process Will Be. You Can Even Go So Far As To Ask By What Date The Company Is Hoping To Fill The Position, What The Preferred Follow-Up Communication Method Would Be, And Would It Be Okay For Your To Check In

With Them Again. These Are All Important Elements You Want To Be Clear On Before Exiting Your Interview.

2. Be Efficient And Responsive - If, During Your Interview, You Indicated That You Would Be Sending Along A List Of Your Personal And Professional References, Then Indeed Do Not Delay. Immediately Sending Along Your References Indicates To Your Interviewers That You Are Organized, And Are Responsive In A Timely Manner, Which Are Remarkably Positive Attributes That Your Interviewer Will Take Note Of And Remember.

3. Be Patient - If Your Interviewer Indicated That It Would Be Fine For You To Check In Following The Interview, And That You Could Do So In About A Week's Time, Be Certain To Do Just That - Check Back And Follow Up A Week Later, Not The Next Day Or Two Days Later. You Do Not Want To Appear Desperate And Impatient, And Surely You Want To Respect The Requests Of Your Employment Interviewer.

4. Say Thank You - The Day After Your Interview, Be Certain To Send Along A Brief Thank-You Email To Your Interviewer, And Follow Up With A Hard Copy Thank You Note To Be Delivered Within Three Business Days. This Is Remarkably Professional, And Very Important To Your Interview Process.

5. Personal Follow-Up Letters - In Addition To A Typical Thank You Note, Sending Along A Personalized Letter To Each Of Your Interviewers Reiterating Your Skillset And Career Accomplishments, And Indicating How They Can Be Linked To The Company's Current Goals And Objectives, Will Surely Make You Shine In The Eyes Of Your Interviewers. In Addition, This Letter Is An Ideal Tool For Enhancing Interview Responses That You Were Unable To Address Fully, Or Even Advising On Your Additional Accomplishments And Achievements That You Were Unable To Discuss At All During The Personal Interview. Further, You Can Utilize These Letters To Perhaps Elaborate On One Of The Informative Details You Learned

About The Company During Your Interview. Perhaps Your Interviewer Discussed Other Areas In The Industry Where The Company Would Like To Branch Out And Expand. You Can Dedicate A Portion Of Your Letter To Explaining How You Would Address That Issue, And Streamline Your Own Knowledge And Efforts To Accomplish This Very Task. Certainly This Is An Ideal Way To Showcase Your Skills, Talents, And Surely Your Professional Enthusiasm.

6. Additional Due Diligence - Although Your Interview Has Been Completed, Take The Initiative To Research And Learn More About The Company Putting Focus On Some Of The Areas Of The Company That Were Discussed In Your Interview. Gathering Additional Company Information, And Preparing A Handful Of New Questions To Ask Will Prove To Be Very Useful In Any Follow-Up Interviews You May Engage In Down The Road. This Technique Indicates To The Hiring Personnel That You Did Not Lose Interest In The Position When Your Interview Was

Over, But Rather Continued To Acquaint Yourself With The Company, And Further Prepare Yourself For Any Additional Interviews.

7. Get The Good Word Out There - If You Happen To Have Any Contacts Or Acquaintances That May Know Your Interviewer, Or May Know Someone In The Higher Chain Of Command In The Company, Don't Hesitate To Ask Them To Reach Out And Put A Good Word In For You. These Types Of References Can Influence A Potential Employer's Decision, And Can Possibly Be A Fine Line Difference Between Losing Out On The Job And Being Hired.

Overall, It Is Every Bit As Important To Give Close Attention And Dedication To Your Actions Following Your Interview, As It Is During The Interview. As Explained Above, There Is No Way Of Knowing If A Candidate Is Going To Work Out, Or If The Company Is Going To Have Additional Employment Needs Going Forward. Being Professional, Courteous, Gracious, Accepting, And Diligent With Your "After

Interview" Presentation Is An Important Element Of The Overall Interviewing Process. Don't Fret. Interviewing Is A Professional Way Of Grooming Oneself For That Perfect Job, And Even If You Do Not Get Hired The First, Second, Or Even Third Time Out Of The Gate, Just Know That Each Time Out You Are Perfecting Your Interviewing Skills, Which Is Ultimately Beneficial To Your Much Needed Interpersonal Skills In Any Position You Will Ultimately Hold, For Any Company.

Chapter 18: Selling Yourself; An Elevator Pitch

Much Like Sales, Public Speaking, And Teaching, Interviewing Is An Art That Requires Practice. You Must Use All Of Your Resources Humanly Possible To Get The Recruiter Or Hiring Manager To Like You. You Can Be Flirtatious And Outgoing, Being Careful Not To Cross Any Professional Lines And Boundaries, Name Drop, Giving Reference And Insight To Your Network, Even Make Prophetic Oaths About What You Will Bring To The Table If Hired. However, All Of This Must Be Backed By Your Professional Work History And Experience; Otherwise, You Will Continue Down The Dark, Government-Funded-Road Of Unemployment.

Like You'll Hear In Many Of My Courses, We, As Recruiters And Hiring Managers, Are Only Looking To Assess Two Things When Interviewing; Your Hard And Soft Skills. To Summarize Quickly, Hard Skills Are Technical Or Quantifiable. They're

Taught Through Repetition, Reading, Or Observing. Your Soft Skills Are More Innate; Skills That Are Learned Through Experience, Development, And Metacognition. Traits Like How You Communicate Or How Creative And Innovative You Are. When The Question Is Asked At The Beginning Of An Interview, "Can You Tell Me A Little About Yourself?" It's Not Because We Don't Know Who You Are. We've Had Your Resume And Application For Quite Some Time Before Deciding If We Had Enough Time In Our Busy Schedule To Meet New People That Day. We Ask Because We Want To Observe Your Soft Skills While You Describe And Tell Us About Your Hard Skills. The Best Way To Do This Is To Create An Elevator Pitch, A Ten-Thousand-Foot View Of Who You Are And Why We As An Organization Need You.

I Read Once That The Term "Elevator Pitch", As You Probably Guessed It, Comes From The Situation Of Someone Pitching An Idea To A Person On An Elevator But Not Having Much Time To "Wow" Or

"Woo" Them. Elevator Rides Tend To Be Short, Around One To Two Minutes, Which Doesn't Leave Much Time For You To Convince Someone Of A Product, Idea, Or Way Of Life. This Is Why You Must Practice Your Elevator Pitch And Create One That Sells Your Abilities To The Fullest. If You Need Help Creating An Elevator Pitch, My Courses Are Designed To Teach You How To Tailor One That Specifically Targets Your Hard And Soft Skills, Making Sure You Open With A Valuable Impression At Any Interview.

The Thing To Remember, If You Remember Nothing Else From This Chapter When In An Interview, Try Not To Open Up With Listing Your Accolades Like A Soliloquy. We Have Your Resume And Know Where You've Worked And For How Long. Talk About Your Experiences Not On Your Resume. Give Dates And Times When Telling Stories. Most Importantly, Give Names As Reference Points In Case They Decide To Do A Professional Reference Check When Hiring You. If You Need More Help In Creating An Elevator Pitch, Contact

Me. I Give Personal One-On-One Interview Training And Resume Building Sessions.

Chapter 19: Main Types Of Interviews

To Make Things Even More Interesting You Should Be Aware That All Interviews Are Not The Same. Different People Conduct Interviews In Different Ways And There Are Different Types Of Interviews As Well. What This Means Is That There Is No One Perfect And Universal Approach To Every Interview.

To Help You Prepare For Any Interview You Might Run Across, Here Are Some Of The Most Common Interview Types. The Interview You Actually Go Out On Will Probably Be One Of These Type. Or. It Might Be A Blend Of Two Or More Of These Types. Either Way, Once You Understand Them You Can Prepare For Them And Do Quite Well.

Here Are The Most Popular Interview Styles / Types:

Screening Interviews

These Are Mostly Interviews Done Over The Phone To Find Out Additional Information Or To See If The Person Is Still

Interested In The Job. There Also Might Be A Bit Of Confusion About Something On The Resume Or Specific Questions That Need To Be Answered Before The Process Moves Forward To An Actual Interview.

These Are Common When Applicant Live A Considerable Distance From Where The Regular Interviews Take Place Or To Reduce The Number Of Applicants To Be Considered For The Full Interviews.

These Are Very Short Interviews, Generally Less Than A Half Hour And Sometimes Much Less. Applicants Finding Themselves At This Point Should Be Encouraged That They Have Made It This Far. This Usually Means That They Have Met The Minimum Qualifications And At Least Are Being Considered At This Time. While This "Pre-Interview" Does Not Always Lead To A Full Interview, It Is Still Considered An Encouraging Sign.

Telephone Or Skype Interviews

When Applicants Come From All Over The Country, Or Whenever Travel Becomes An Issue For Either The Company Of The Applicants, Sometimes Telephone

Interviews Are Given First To Make Sure Only The Most Qualified People Are Flown In For Further Interviews.

These Interviews Last Longer And Are Pretty Much The Same As In-Person Interviews As Far As Questions And Information Exchange. The Main Difference Is That Unless The Interview Is Done Over Skype Or A Webinar Platform The Interviewer Cannot See You And You Cannot See The Interviewer.

One Downside To A Telephone Interview Is That You Have No Idea How Serious The Interviewer Actually Is Or Whether There Is Anyone Else Listening In Or In The Room With The Interviewer. Though They Are Supposed To Inform You, The Interview Might Also Be Recorded As Well.

As With Any Interview, Be Careful What You Say And How You Say It. One Advantage To A Phone Interview Is That You Can Have Your Notes Opened Or Your Computer On And Search For Information As You Need It. This Is Not A Substitute For Good Preparation But It Can Help If You

Are Asked Something You Were Not Prepared For.

Though There Are Exceptions Telephone Interviews Usually Do Not End With An Offer Of Employment. Instead They Are Just The First Interview Of Two Or Three. Most Of The Time Applicants That Pass The First Interview Will Be Brought In For A Face-To-Face Interview Or Two Before Any Offers Are Made.

Standard Interview

This Is The Most Common Type Of Interview And Therefore The One You Are Most Likely To Face, Especially For A First Interview. This Is Where The Interviewer Goes Over Your Resume And Asks You A Series Of Questions Designed To Get You To Open Up About Yourself, Your Education And Experience. If Is A Free Flowing Of Information Mostly Initiated By The Interviewer.

These Are The Easiest Kinds Of Interviews To Prepare And Practice For Because You Just Have To Think About Answers To The Most Common Interview Questions. Once You Have Those Answers Committed To

Memory It Is All About Appearance, Demeanor And Impressions.

Standard Interviews Generally Take Between 30 Minutes To An Hour And You Might Get A Little Tour Of The Business Is There Is Time. It Is A "Get To Know You" Type Of Interview That Gives The Interviewer A Chance To See The Personality Behind The Resume. It Is Also Where They Get To Evaluate Your Appearance As Well To Make Sure It Fits Their Corporate Culture.

Behavioral Interview

These Interviews Concentrate On Behavioral Aspect Of The Applicant And Are Usually Encountered I Second Or Third Interviews. This Is Where They Ask You How You Would React To Certain Situations And How You Get Along With Others. They Will Ask You About Your Communication Skills And Other "Soft" Skills.

These Interviews Also Dive Into Your Values, Morals And Decision Making Capabilities As Well. Because Of This Be Very Careful How You Answer These Types

Of Questions. They Are Designed To Get You To Share Information That They Might Not Be Allowed To Ask You Under The Law. Answer As Honestly As You Can While Framing Your Answer In An Acceptable Manner And Keep The Answers Short And Sweet.

Situation Interview

This Is Where They Sit You Down And Ask You How You Would Handle Certain Situations. They Ask You What You Would Do In This Situation Or How You Would Handle That Situation. These Questions Are Designed Not Only To Test Your Knowledge But Also Your Decision Making Skills, Your Values, Your Honesty And Integrity.

Sometimes These Questions Might All Seem Very Innocent But They Are Designed To See How You Would React To Certain Requests, Pressures And Situations. What You Do And How You React Often Will Give Them A Great Deal Of Knowledge About Who You Are As A Person As Well As An Applicant.

They Are Useful Because Most Interviewers Realize That Most Applicants Practice The Routine Questions And Have Pre-Designed Or "Canned" Answers. But These Situational Questions Are Not Easily Practiced For And Reveal More Of A True Reflection Of The Applicant.

Case Study Interview

Similar To A Situational Interview, A Case Study Interview Is Where They Show You Something That Already Happened And Ask You What You Might Have Done Differently Or Better In Order To Get A Better Result.

These Interviews Are Designed To Test Several Things At Once. They Are Testing Your Knowledge, Your Decision Making, How Well Or Poorly You Can Evaluate A Situation And You Problem Solving And Interpersonal Skills. All In One Simple Exercise.

The Key To Performing Well In These Interviews Is Being Able To Process Information And Uncover All The Details. If Something Appear Missing, It Might Have Been Left Out Intentionally To See If You

Would Ask. Evaluate Everything, Ask Questions As Needed And Rely On Your Knowledge And Expertise To Help You Arrive At The Best Possible Answer.

Often Times There Is No One Really Right Answer. The Interviewer Is Less Concerned With The Answer You Gave As They Are About How You Arrived At That Answer. If Your Deductive Skills Were Good And Your Reasoning Is Sound, That Is What's Important. How You Arrived At Your Decision Is What They Are Really Most Interested In.

Case Study Interviews Are Usually Reserved For Advanced Interviews And Not First Interviews. A Possible Exception Is When Someone Well Known With A Great Reputation Is Brought In To Talk With People Before Being Hired. In Those Case They Might Dispense With The Formalities And Get Right To The Important Stuff.

Presentation Interview

Almost Always Reserved For Advanced Interviews This Is Where You Are Asked To Give A Presentation On Some Skill Or

Activity Directly Relevant To The Job You Are Being Considered For. If You Applied For A Sales Position, For Example, You Might Be Asked To Prepare A Powerpoint Presentation On The Latest Product And Present It To A Group Of People.

This Is Aimed At Looking At How Well You Speak To Others And How Well You Related To Different People. They Will See How You React To Interruptions And Questions And Who Well You Stay On Track And On Message.

If A Specific Skill Is Required They Might Ask You To Demonstrate That Skill As Well In Front Of A Group Of People. If You Want To Be A Teaching You Might Be Asked To Present A Lesson To The Group. If You Are Applying For A Position Dealing With Customers, They Might Ask You To Do Some Role Playing To Demonstrate Your Approach And Soft Skills.

These Interviews Are Given To See How You Perform And Communicate With Other People. If You Are Applying For A Position That Has High Visibility And A Lot Of Communication Skills, This Might Be

The Type Of Interview You Encounter Near The End Of The Interview Process.

Demonstration Interview

This Interview Is Almost The Same As A Presentation Interview Except That It Is More Geared Or Aimed At Demonstrating One's Skills. For Example, If You Wanted To Hire A Piano Player For Your Club, You Would Want To Hear Them Play A Few Songs. If You Were Looking For Graphics Artist, You Might Want To See Them Create Something For Your Company At The Interview.

Demonstration Skills Are Great For People Whose Skills Are Top Notch. If Your Skills Are The Best You Can Truly Shine Your Way Through This Interview With Little Or No Effort. But If Your Skills Are Not Top Notch, This Interview Could Very Well Reveal That To Everyone.

So If You Are Applying For A Job Requiring Specific Skill Sets, Do Your Best To Refine Them Just In Case You Are Asked To Demonstrate Them During This Type Of Interview. I\Even If It Never Comes To That Your Improved Skills Will Help You Do A

Better Job Once You Are Hired Anyway. So It's A Win-Win For Everyone.

Panel Or Group Interview

These Are The Interviews That Strike Fear In The Hearts Of Applicants Far And Wide. This Is Where You Sit Or Stand In A Room And Are Interviewed By Several People At The Same Time. Sometimes This Is One Way Of Having Multiple People Interview You At The Same Time Saving Time In The Process. Other Times It Is Just To See How Well You Perform Under More Pressure And How You Can Relate To A Group Of People Rather Than Just One.

These Interviews Can Be Difficult Because Of The Different Personalities Sitting Around The Same Table. There Might Be Interruptions Or Several People Might Be Talking At The Same Time. This Could Even Be Done On Purpose To See How You React Under Such Chaos.

I Have Always Found That It Works Best To Signal Out One Or Two Of The Most Difficult People As You Perceive Them And Then Concentrate On Them. The Reason Being If You Can Satisfy The Most

Demanding People You Stand A Good Chance Of Impressing The Others As Well. It Doesn't Work The Other Way Around.

This Type Of Interview Can Really Make You Shine If You Handle It Well. But If You Are Easily Intimidated You Had Better Deal With That First As Those Feelings Can Get You In Trouble Fast. But Keep In Mind That If They Truly Are Considering You For The Job, Which They Probably Are, They Will Give You A Fair Shot And Are Just Wondering How Well You Can Control And Command The Room.

Of All The Types Of Interviews, This Is The One Where Being Confident In Yourself And Your Abilities Really Helps. If You Believe In Yourself And What You Are Capable Of It Won't Make A Difference Whether You Are Talking To One Person Or 50. Your Confidence Will Show Through And You Will Do Just Fine.

Luncheon Interview

While This Might Seem To Be The Most Comfortable And Innocent Of Interviews, You Had Better Be Careful And Bring

You're A Game Because It Can Also Be The Most Dangerous!

Interviewing Over Lunch Or Dinner Is Meant To Get You To Relax So The Interviewer Can Get Closer To The "Real You". They Want You To Lower Your "Applicant Persona" And Be More Yourself And Perhaps Share More Of You Than You Really Should.

During The Meal You Will Discuss Yourself And The Company And You Will Answer Pretty Much The Same Questions That You Would Be Asked Had You Been Sitting In An Office With The Person Sitting Across The Desk From You. That Part Is Pretty Straightforward. It Is The Personal Questions Or The Small Talk That Can Get You In Trouble.

Keep The Conversation Contained To "Safe" Areas. Safe Areas Avoid Politics, Sex, Religion, Morals, Values And Other Personal Areas. Also Stay Clear Of Offensive Or Off-Color Jokes And Inappropriate Comments About Anything. In Other Words, Talk Just Like You Would If Your Two Grandmothers And Your

Minister Were Sitting At The Table With You.

Order Something Easy To Eat That Is Not Messy Or Easy To Spill. Chances Are You Will Be A Bit Nervous So Stay Away From Soup. Also Stay Away From Finger Food Such As Ribs Which Are Messy To Eat. Have A Burger Or A Sandwich Or Something Safe And Easy To Eat.

As Far As Beverages Are Concerned, Never Order Wine Or Anything Containing Any Kind Of Alcohol Even If The Other Person Has Ordered That And Encourages You To Do The Same. Stick With Water, Soda Or Iced Tea. After All, You Want To Keep Your Head Clear And Capable Of Controlling What It Is Saying And Thinking. Alcohol And Interviews Definitely Do Not Mix!

Stress Interview

This Is A Strange Type Of Interview Because It Seems Like Everyone There Is Looking To Make You Fail. People Might Be Hostile Towards You, Argue With You At Every Opportunity And Make You Have To Work Hard To Make Every Point Or Win Any Exchange. You Might Feel That It Is

You Against Everyone Else Because That Is Exactly How They Want It To Be.

In These Types Of Interviews It Is Important To Understand That They Really Do Want You To Succeed. But In Order To Pick Someone Will Succeed In A High Pressure Or High Stress Job They Need To Make Reasonably Sure The Person Is Capable Of Handling These High Stress Or Uncomfortable Situations When The Occur. So Instead Of Trying To Determine Whether You Can Or Can't Deal With Them, They Create One.

The Important Thing Is To Remain Calm And In Control Even Though People Might Be Doing Their Best To Frustrate Or Distract You. Stay On Point And Stay On Message. If Necessary Stop Talking And Take A Breath And Then Try To Reassert Control Over The Situation. When People Interrupt You Deal With It Calmly And Respectfully And Do Not Allow Yourself To Be Distracted. Just Tell The People Who Are Interrupting You That You Will Answer Their Question Once You Have Finished Answering The Current Question.

If People Are Rude Or Use Offensive Language, Do Not Reduce Yourself To Their Level. Always Treat Everyone With Dignity And Respect. If It Gets Too Much, You Might Want To Comment On The Language And Ask That They Refrain From Using It. Use Your Judgment On That One Although They Might Be Trying To See How You Will Respond To Poor Language.

Sometimes You Might Think That Thing Were Taken A Bit Too Far Or You Might Be Too Offended By What Had Taken Place. When You Get To That Point You Might Want To Ask Yourself If These People Are Just Playing Roles In The Process Or If They Really Are Arrogant And Offensive Jerks. If They Are Just Playing A Role That Is One Thing. But If They Really Are Arrogant And Insensitive Jerks You Might Want To Re-Visit Whether Or Not You Really Want To Work For A Company That Would Employ Such People.

Chances Are Any Interview You Encountered Will Be One Of These Types Or At Worst A Blend Of A Couple Of Different Types. But Now You Know What

To Expect And What Is Behind Each Type Of Interview. You Know That Questions Might Not Always Be What They Seem And You Know That You Should Be Careful Of What You Say And Why You Said It.

If You Move Forward With The Approach That Every Word You Say And Every Action You Take Should Bring You Closer To Landing The Job, Then You Should Be Just Fine. Just Keep On Point And On Message And Do Not Allow Others To Distract You From What You Want To Accomplish Or Trick You Into Saying Something You Shouldn't.

If You Can Manage All Of That, You Will Do Just Fine.

Chapter 20: Popular Interview Questions

Generally Speaking There Are Going To Be Certain Questions That Arise At Your Interview That You Can Pretty Much Expect To Get Asked At Any Other Interview You Attend. The Great Thing About This Is The Fact That You Can Rehearse Your Answers To These Questions And With Enough Practice They Will Flow Off Your Head Without Much Struggle.

These Questions Are Likely To Be Fired At All Candidates Applying For The Job So Although They May Sound Personal To You. These Are Pretty Standard Interview Questions.

I Have Chosen To Isolate The Popular Interview Questions From The Tough Questions To Give You A Chance To Focus On Them Individually. You Have To Bear In Mind That These Examples Are Based On The Responses That I Would Consider Giving But They Are Not Engraved In Stone

And You Will Need To Adapt The Answers To Your Situation.

Here We Go:

"Tell Me About Yourself"

This Isn't As Straight Forward To Answer As It Might Seem. Don't Start Rambling On About Where You Grew Up And Where You Went To School Or How Much You Love Watching The Super Sport On The Tv. That Isn't What The Interviewer Is Looking To Hear.

This Is Your Chance To Sell Yourself (Your Personal, Professional And Business Profiles) As Discussed In Chapter 2.

For Example You Could Say "On A Personal Level I Am A Very <u>Organized</u> Person With <u>Drive</u> And Always <u>Motivated</u> By New Challenges. I Give Extra Effort To Important Matters As Well As The Little Things [**Energy**]. The Success In My Career So Far Has Been Driven Largely By My <u>Desire</u> To Get Along With Others [**Chemistry**] Which Has Enabled Me Build Trustworthy And Lasting Relationships [**Team Player**]. My Ability To Effectively Talk And Write To Those Above And Below

Me Has Also Endeared Me To All My Colleagues". [**Communication Skills**]

"On The Professional Level, I Take Pride For The Fact That I Deal Diligently And Honestly With All [**Integrity**]. I Also Follow Up On All My Assignments To Successful Completion [**Reliable**] And Always Weighing The Pro And Cons Of Each Possible Solution" [**Analytical**].

"I Respect Company Procedures And I Always Keep My Boss And Juniors In The Loop On Any Project Whilst Being On The Look Out To Improve Efficiency In Resource Allocation". Lastly, I Enjoy Finding A New Prospect, Working With It And Closing The Deal, Carrying Out The Process From Start To Finish". [Business Profile]

Please Note That Your Desirable Traits Are Cleverly Intertwined Into Your Answer. This Is Who You Are And What Makes You Tick.

Sometimes Your Interviewer Might Ask About Specifics And Again You Should Pick Out Points That Relate To Your Desirable Traits And The Job You Are Applying For.

What Is The Most Enjoyable Part Of Your Current Job?

This Is A Fairly Straight Forward Question But Has A Bit Of A Double Meaning. Obviously There Are Going To Be Parts Of Your Existing Job That You Don't Like Doing – Or You Wouldn't Be Applying For This New Position Would You, But Your Job Can't Be That Great Either Or You Wouldn't Be Applying For This Job!

Don't Get Led Down This Route, Just Answer Something Along The Lines Of:

"My Current Job Is Great And I Can't Really Put A Finger On Any Part That Is Not Enjoyable. I Realize That Every Aspect Of This Job Has Helped To Groom My Communication Skills, Drive, Confidence, Analytical Abilities And My Business Acumen Etc. All These Aspects Have Helped Me Want To Contribute At A Higher Levels Whilst Furthering My Career" And Leave It At That.

Note That Again We Are Using Key Profile Traits To Answer This Question. Look At Each Question As An Opportunity To Sell Your Desirable Traits.

Tell Us About The Biggest Challenge You've Ever Faced In Your Career?

Oh Wow, This Is A Really Great Question To Help You Shine! You Are More Than Likely To Be Asked This Question And It Is A Really Great Opportunity For You To Blow Your Own Trumpet Or So To Speak. It Is An Opportunity To Sell Your Achievement Profile. Pick A Challenge Where You Have Been Successful And Explain How You Overcame The Challenge And The Outcome. Give An Example Which Should Follow The Following Process As Outlined In Chapter 2.

A) **State The Problem:** What Was The Situation? Was It Typical Of Your Job, Or Had Something Gone Wrong? Be Cautious Of Appointing Blame.

B) **Isolate Relevant Background Information:** What Specific Knowledge Or Education Were You Armed With To Tackle This Dilemma?

C) **List Your Key Qualities:** What Professional Skills And Personal Behavior Traits Did You Bring In To Play To Solve The Problem?

D) **Recall The Solution.** How Did Things Turn Out In The End? (If The Problem Did Not Have A Successful Resolution, Do Not Use It As An Example)

E) **Determine What The Solution Was Worth:** Quantify The Solution In Terms Of The Money Earned, Money Served, Or Time Served. Specify Your Role As A Team Member Or As A Lone Gun, As The Facts Demand.

- Now Rehearse Your Story Until You Can Tell It In 60 Seconds Flat!

This Question Can Also Be Used By The Interviewer To Gauge What You Consider To Be A Challenge So This Is A Bit Of A Crafty One As Well.

Why Do You Want To Leave Your Present Job?

This Is A Fairly Of A Dim Question Really As The Chances Of The Interviewer Getting A Straight Answer Are Fairly Limited.

Let's Face It If The Job Your In Doesn't Pay Very Well And You Want More Money You Are Going To Be Looking For A New Job. It Might Be That Your Current Boss Is A Complete Idiot And You Don't Like Him, It

Could Be You Can't Stand Working With Billy In Accounts, Let's Face It You Aren't Going To Say Any Of These...Or Are You?.

A Standard Response Along The Lines Of "I Feel That I Have Outgrown My Current Position And My Contribution As Part Of A Team Could Be Put To Much Better Use With A Larger Company Where I Can Explore New Areas Of Responsibility And Expand My Skills Further. I Am Really Interested In [**Outline Areas Of Responsibilities The New Job Has To Offer**]……..But My Existing Employer Doesn't Have The Resources To Let Me Advance In This Area" And Leave It At That. Just Try Not To Be Negative About The Job You Are Leaving It Doesn't Look Good.

What Is Your Present Boss Like?

Another Question Posed By Interviewers To Gauge Your Loyalty And Integrity. It Is Not A Good Idea To Be Critical About Any Of The Employers You Have Ever Worked For.

Let's Face It Very Few Of Us Actually Like Our Bosses (Well Most Of Us Just Appease

Them By Telling Them What They Want To Hear), After All Why Wouldn't You Want To Be Best Buddies With A Person Who Holds You Career Prospects In Their Hands!

If You Get Asked This Question The Most Appropriate Reply Is "I Like My Boss And Get On Very Well With Him, I Respect His Experience And He Is Good At His Job".

You Really Don't Need To Expand Any Further On This Issue At Interview Stage. You Have To Remember That The Person Interviewing You May Well, At Some Point In The Near Future, Become Your Boss And They Are Weighing Up Your Loyalty And Integrity.

What Do You Think This Job Entails?

Now When You Are Applying For A New Job The Chances Are You Are Going To Know Something About What Your New Job Would Entail. For Example, If The Job Is An Accounting Role And You Are An Accountant, You Will Know What Sort Of Work You Are Going To Be Involved With. In Any Case You Will Have Been Given A Brief Description Of The Job Role And

What Responsibilities It Carries With It So You Should Be Able To Make A Fairly Calculated Guess At What The Job Entails.

Again Take Time To Sell Your Desirable Professional And Personality Profiles Which Makes You Stand Out As An Accountant.

What Do You Know This Organisation?

Now Having Done Your Research And Read Up About What The Company Is Involved In, Its Products, Its Services, Its Turnover And Its Strategy. You Will Really Impress Your Interviewer If You Are Able To Show That You Have Done Some Research About Their Company.

As Previously Mentioned People Like To Think That If You Are Really Eager To Work For Them You Will Have Done Some Research About What They Do And How They Do It.

So Let's Say You Are Applying For A Job With Someone Like Nestle You Could Say Something Like "I Notice That You Are The World's Largest Food And Drink Company The World Who Operate A "Fair Trade Policy" When Purchasing Your Goods From

Third World Countries I Have To Say That I Am Very Supportive Of This And It's Nice To Work For An Employer Who Cares About The Impact Their Business Has On People In The Developing World".

What Made You Apply For This Job And Why Do You Want It**?**

This Is A Bit Of A Double Edged Question. Your Interviewer Isn't Necessarily Looking For An Answer Here That Is Straight Forward – You Know You Are Applying For The Job Because You Think You Would Enjoy Doing It, The Package Is Right And You Think You Would Be Able To Advance Your Career With This Firm – But The Interviewer Wants To See If There Are Some Specifics That Really Attract You To It (Other Than The £ 4,000 Per Month And A Company House!).

So Depending On What The Role Is, You Could Use An Answer Such As "I Am A Very Well Organised Person And This Role Involves Exceptional Management Skills. I Thrive Under Pressure And It Makes Me Perform To My Full Ability Which Makes Me Think That I Would Really Enjoy It".

Obviously You Can Tailor This Answer To Whatever Role You Are Applying For.

What Qualities Do You Think You Can Bring To This Job Position?

Again, You Know That You Can Do This Job And That Is Why You Have Applied For It. Not Only Do You Know That You Can Do The Job, You Will Do It Better Than Anyone Else So You Will Be Aware Of The Qualities You Are Going To Bring To This Business. You Will Have Reviewed The Job Specifics And The Key Responsibilities So You Will Be Able To Select Several Areas Where You Feel Your Qualities Will Stand Out.

Perhaps You Could Therefore Give An Answer Along The Lines Of "I Have Experience Working In The Complaints Department Where A Sympathetic Touch Is Required Dealing With Disgruntled Customers. I Am Very Tactful And Am Able To Defuse Situations Using My Personal Skills".

How Long Would You Expect To Work For Our Organisation?

Let's Face It No Employer Wants To Go Through The Hassle And Cost Of Hiring A

New Candidate If The Candidate Only Stays With Them For 6 Months And Then Decides To Apply To Another Firm. The Recruitment Process Is A Long An Expensive One Especially Where Agencies Are Used To Introduce The Candidate. This Could Cost Your Potential Employer As Much As 30% Of Your First Year's Package! It's Probably A Good Idea Therefore To Intimate That You Would Like To Work For This Firm For Several Years Minimum And You Could Provide An Answer Along The Lines Of "I Like The Way Your Company Is Continuing To Expand And I Would Like To Be Part Of That On A Long Term Basis. So I Would Like To Think That I Could Continue To Work For You For A Lengthy Period Of Time Providing My Career Continues To Progress".

What's Your Greatest Strength?

Only You Can Answer This Question, But It Is A Question That Will More Than Likely Be Asked, After All, The Interviewer Wants To Know What You Are Good At. This Question Gives You Pretty Much An Open Mandate To Really Show Off, Or So To

Speak. When Answering This Question Try And Provide Strengths That Relate To The Role That You Are Applying For, So If The Job Requires The Need To Be Organised And A Good Team Leader Provide These As Strengths Within Your Answer. Remember The Universally Admired Behavioral Traits.

What Is Your Biggest Weakness?

A Tricky Question This One Is, After All No One Wants To Show Their Weaknesses But We All Have Them.

Did You Know That All Humanity Is Perfect! What Others Say Is A Weakness Could Be A Strength Given A Change In Environment. Therefore A Weakness Should Be Defined In Relation To A Particular Situation.

For Example, A Loud Mouthed Fellow In A Consulting Firm Or A Hospital Is Not A Welcome Idea. However, This Same Fellow Employed By An Entertainment Firm Could Be An A1 Performer.

The Most Comprehensive Way Of Dealing With This Question Is To Try And Turn The "Negative" Into A "Positive".

So You Could Perhaps Say "My Biggest Weakness Is Being Empathetic To My Friends And Colleagues Even When They Clearly Deserve The Outcome Of Whatever It Is They Have Done. But Once I Have Shown Empathy It Always Gives Me A Real Sense Of Satisfaction".

Where Do You See Yourself In Five Years' Time?

Don't Say As I Have Heard So Many Times "Sitting In Your Job!" Although I Have A Sense Of Humour Most Interviewers Don't. The Remark Often Has An Element Of Truth Hanging In The Background And You Don't Want Your Interviewer Thinking You Are Potentially A Threat To His Or Her Job In The Future. I Am Sure You Will Have Ideas About Where You Want To Be In A Few Years Most People, Whether They Put Them Down On Paper Or Not, Have A Good Idea Of Their Long Term Career Objectives.

Try And Answer The Question Positively But Not Too Arrogantly – Perhaps You Could Say Offer An Answer Such As "I Have Always Been Very Career Minded And

Ambitious. I Would Like To Keep Progressing Up The Career Ladder And I Feel That Your Organization Will Be Able To Offer Me That Opportunity".

What Would Your Work Colleagues Say About You?

This Question Provides Another Opportunity For You To Demonstrate That You Are Easy To Get On With, A Team Player And A Generally Open Person Who Works Well With Other People.

You Could Answer This Question With A Quote Such As "I Am An Organised, Approachable, Dependable, Easy To Get On With Team Member Who Is Always Willing To Offer My Advice Or Assistance To Colleagues Where Needed".

Don't Go Overboard With Your Answer Making Out You Are Something You Are Not – You May Get Away With Stretching The Truth But If You Are Not A "Natural Team Leader" Don't Say You Are!

What Would Your Friends Say About You?

Obviously This Question Is Similar To The Previous One. If You Are A Popular, Kind, Caring Person Who Can Be Counted On

And Would Help A Friend Out At The Drop Of A Hat Then Let Your Interviewer Know.

What Interests Do You Have Outside Of Your Work?

This Will Be A Definite Question (In My Opinion) And Is Posed By Your Interviewer To Try And Ascertain What You Are Like Outside Of Your Working Environment. If You Don't Like Football Or Basketball Don't Say That You Do, Just Provide Honest Answers. There Is Nothing Worse Than Saying You Follow A Sport And Then It Turns Out That The Interviewer Is Mad About The Subject And Starts Asking You A Question You Can't Answer. You Will Look A Fool And Your Honesty Will Be Under Scrutiny!

What Type Of Books Or Publications Do You Like?

This Question Needs And Honest Answer. Just Because You Think The Interviewer Is Looking To Hear You Tell Them That You Have Just Finished "The 7 Habits Of Successful People" And That It Was The Best Read Of Your Life It Isn't A Good Idea To Make It Up.

If You Have Genuinely Read "Nelson Mandela's" Autobiography Or "Stephen Kings" Latest Books Then Tell The Employer What You Enjoyed About Them.

Of Course If You Work Within A Certain Industry And Read The Trade Publications And Have Recently Read An Interesting Article About The Latest "Technology Release" Then By All Means Use This As An Example.

Chapter 21: 10 Must Prepared Interview Questions

Tell Me Of A Time When You Had A Conflict With Your Supervisor/Head?

Tips: This Is A Tricky Question And Such Questions Would Definitely Arrive. Team Leaders Or Supervisors Have A Definite Work Plan In Their Minds Even When They Invite The Team For Discussion. Conflict Is Unavoidable If You Voice Your Opinion. Not All Supervisors Would Like This Situation, However At Times You Could Also Come Out Of This Situation Being A Winner. That Is Exactly What You Need To Tell The Interviewer.

Answer: I Remember This One Time When My Boss Was Not Happy With My Work. He Consistently Criticized Me And This Went On To Getting Worse. Then One Day I Realized My Mistake. Everybody In The Office Would Ask Him About His Health, Family And That How He's Doing. While I Was Only Answering My Boss's Questions Regarding My Health Etc And Not Did Not

Ask How He Was Doing. Realizing This, I Quickly Made Amendments And From That Day On, We Get Along Really Well.

Why Did You Apply For This Job?

Tips: Match Your Skills, Abilities And Qualifications With The Requirements For This Job. You Should Sound As If The Job Was Made For You. If You Have Relevant Experience Then Mentioning That Would Make An Excellent Impression On The Interviewer.

Answer: I Believe My Abilities Are A Best Match For This Job And My Five Years Of Professional Experience In The Same Field Also Provides Me An Edge On Others. I Am Sure That I Can Utilize My Knowledge And Skills To The Best Of My Abilities To Carry Out The Responsibilities Of This Job.

What Made You Choose Our Company?

Tips: Do Your Homework Before Coming To The Interview. All Your Hard Work Would Show In The Information That You Have Gathered. Know What The Current Market Stats Say About The Company And What Recent New Changes They Have Done.

Answer: This Company Promises Professional Growth And Compensations Much More Than Its Competitors. My Research Shows That The Recent Changes In Its Organizational Structure Will Greatly Benefit Its Workers And Consumers. I Will Be More Than Pleased To Be A Part Of This Progressive Company.

What Starting Compensations Are You Expecting?

Tips: You Have To Be Honest Otherwise You Could Lose This Opportunity As Employers Sometimes Check On Your Employment History And Salary Packages. Your Information Should Be Not Only Correct But Also Should Match Your Entire Profile. There Is No Way Else To Go About This Question But To Be Straight And Honest.

Answer: My Salary Package At Xyz As A Senior Blah Blah Was Blah Blah. I Also Got Medical For Parents, Spouse And Children Up To Blah Blah. I Got Reimbursement Of Travel Expenses; Two Leave Fares Annually, One Bonus A Year…. Blah Blah

What Do You Think Is The Salary Package Suitable For This Job?

Tips: You Should Know About The Current Salary Packages For The Particular Job In Different Companies And Preferably In The Same Company Where You Are Applying. Come Up With A Salary Range And Think About Your Own Range As Well.

Answer: I Know That The Average Salary Range For This Position In The Market Varies From X To Z. I Shall Be Glad To Get Somewhere In Between That.

What Are Your Career Goals?

Tips: You Could Come Up With Short Term And Long Term Goals Whatever You Choose If Not Asked Specifically. Your Goals Should Involve Achieving The Company's Vision And Help It Grow. But An Entry Level Person Saying That He Aims To Becoming The Company's Ceo Would Sound Too Much. Be Reasonable And Even If You Aim Big, Your Timing Matters A Lot.

Answer: I Want To Excel In My Field And Then Move Within The Company To Learn About Other Departments And Fields.

Once I Become A Master In All, I Would Want To Pursue My Career In Management As Leadership Comes Natural To Me.

Will You Rate Yourself As Being Successful? What Is Your Key To Success?

Tips: Be As Positive And Confident As You Can When You Say That You Think You Are Successful.

This Should Show In Your Attitude. But Keep In Mind To Maintain The Right Balance As You Do Not Want To Sound Over Confident. Also Do Not Answer This Question Humbly As It Will Show Lack Of Self Esteem. Just Be Yourself, Self Assured And Comfortable In Your Shoes.

Answer: Yes, I Would Say Confidently That I Am Successful. I Believe Hard Work And Total Dedication Towards My Job Makes Me Where I Am Today.

What Did You Like The Least About This Job?

Tips: Be Careful While Answering This Question. Do Not Say Anything Bad As You Went Through Your Research For This Role And The Company And You Found

Everything According To Your Requirements. However, If The Interviewer Insists, You Can Come Up With A Polite Answer. You Should Never Mention Anything The Interviewer Would Want To Defend. Anything Minor That Can Be Managed Easily Would Be Okay To Say.

Answer: This Position Is Great To Work For And There Is Absolutely Nothing To Dislike. I Am Most Looking Forward To Working For You On This.

Do You Have Any Questions?

Tips: An Almost A Must Question In Every Interview. Do You Homework Before Coming To The Interview And Be Prepared To Ask A Few Questions. Your Questions Should Show Your Interest In The Job And The Company. Search Up For Recent News Regarding The Company, It Client Base And Anything Else There Is To Know.

Answer: I Wanted To Know If The Recent Merger With Xyz Has Made Any Impact On Your Customer Response.

Could You Give Me One Good Reason To Hire You For This Position?

Tips: You Should Be The Most Suitable Candidate For This Job In Your Mind So That You Are Able To Come Up With A Positive Answer Showing Your Confidence In Yourself. Your Educational Background, Previous Work Experience And Technical Skills Should All Be Laid Out For The Interviewer In A Manner Which Strengthens Your Chances Of Being The Best Candidate For The Job.

Answer: Although There Are A Lot Many People Applying For This Position And All Of Them Must Be Well Qualified But I Assure You That With My Knowledge And Past Experience, I Am The Most Suitable Candidate For This Job. I Thrive For Excellence And With My Passion To Do The Best, I Am Sure I Will Bring More Valuable Contributions To Your Company Than Anyone Else. Blah Blah.

Chapter 22: Types Of Interview Questions

Now That You Understand The Different Types Of Interviews That You May Encounter, There Are Also Different Types Of Questions That You Want To Prepare For. Other Than The Basic, "Tell Me About Yourself" Or "What Are Your Strengths And Weaknesses", You May Also Encounter Questions That Give The Interviewer An Idea Of How You Behave In Particular Situations Or How You Handle Specific Situations.

Answering These Questions May Seem A Bit Difficult Because You Need To Figure Out What The Interviewer Actually Wants To Know, Then You Want To Answer In A Way That Best Fits The Needs Of The Position They Are Looking To Fill. For Example, If You're Interviewing For An Outside Sales Position, The Interviewer May Ask, "Do You Prefer To Work Alone Or With A Team?" There Are Many Ways To Answer This Question, But Answering In A Specific Way Will Greatly Increase Your

Chances Of Getting Hired. First You Need To Figure Out Why The Interviewer Is Asking This Question, And What He Or She Really Wants To Know. Understanding The Job Description Will Greatly Help At This Point. In An Outside Sales Position, You Will Most Likely Be Working Alone For A Majority Of The Time. The Interviewer Wants To Know If You Feel Comfortable With That And If You Can Handle The Position With Minimal Direction. A Good Way To Answer This Question Is To Tell The Interviewer That You Prefer To Work Alone, And Then Explain How You're Able To Take Initiative With Little Assistance Needed. Now That We Have A Better Understanding Of Figuring Out How To Translate Interview Questions, Let's Take A Further Look Into Four Types Of Questions We May Encounter.

Behavioral Questions

Behavioral Questions Focuses On Past Experiences And A Candidate Acted In A Specific Situation. It Works On The Principle "Past Performance Predicts Future Performance". This Type Of

Question Gives The Interviewer A Glimpse Of The Character And Personality Of A Candidate.

Most Candidates Find Behavioral Questions Tough To Answer. You Will Need To Think Back On Your Past Experiences Then Come Up With A Specific Instance When You Exhibited That Behavior. Then You Are Expected To Describe How You Handled That Situation. In The End, Your Answer Should Be Valid And Interesting Enough To Impress The Interviewer. Recalling A Specific Instance Of Your Life Can Be A Bit Difficult When Put On The Spot, Especially During An Interview. Preparing For Behavioral Questions Beforehand Is The Key To Success In Such Interviews.

Now That We Understand The Meaning Of A Behavioral Question, Let's Take A Look At Common Behavioral Questions That You May Be Asked:

Describe A Time When You Were Wrong.

Tell Me About A Time When You Dealt With An Angry Customer.

Describe A Time When You Disagreed With Your Supervisor.

Share An Example Of How You Were Able To Motivate Employees Or Coworkers.

Tell Me About A Time When One Of Your Coworkers Was Not Pulling His Or Her Weight. How Did You Handle It?

Give An Example Of A Goal You Reached And How You Achieved It.

Describe A Stressful Situation At Work, And How You Handled It.

Give An Example Of A Time When You Had To Make A Difficult Decision.

Give An Example Of A Goal You Didn't Meet And How You Handled It.

Tell Me About A Time When You Went Above And Beyond Your Duties.

Behavioral Questions Differ From Position To Position. Be Prepared To Bring Out Your Personality In Every Answer But Don't Forget To Figure Out What The Interviewer Actually Wants To Know, So That Way You Are Able To Answer These Questions In Your Favor.

Situational Questions

Situational Questions Focus On Potential Future Events And How A Candidate Would Handle A Specific Situation. These Questions Involve Difficult Situations And Problem Solving To Assess A Candidates Ability To Handle A Specific Job. There Can Be An Infinite Number Of Circumstances And This Is What Makes Situational Questions So Challenging. Below Are A Few Examples Of Situational Questions That You May Be Asked:

What Would You Do If You Realized You Weren't Going To Complete An Important Project By The Deadline?

What Would You Do If You Knew Your Supervisor Was Completely Wrong About A Decision He Asked You To Carry Out?

If You Were Give Multiple Tasks To Complete At Once, How Would You Prioritize?

If You Were Asked To Lead A Team With A New Project And They Disagreed With Your Ideas, How Would You Handle It?

If A Member On Your Team Is Underperforming, What Would You Do?

What Would You Do If You Were Paired Up With A Coworker To Complete A Project That You Did Not Get Along With?

If Your Performance Review Describes Your Work As Unsatisfactory, How Would You React?

If Your Supervisor Asked You To Carry Out A Task That You Did Not Understand Or Did Not Have The Skills To Complete, How Would You Handle The Situation?

If You Completed Your Portion Of A Project Earlier Than Your Team Members And Still Had Time To Spare, What Would You Do?

If One Of Your Coworkers Has A Negative Attitude In The Workplace, What Would You Do?

Situational Questions Will Test Your Decision Making Skills And Will Allow The Interviewer To Have An Idea Of How You Would Fit In The Position. Before You Answer, Think About How The Interviewer Would Want The Ideal Candidate To React In Each Situation.

Tell Me About Yourself

Most Interviewers Start Off With This Question. It Is One Of The Most Frequently

Asked Questions Which Can Be Answered In Multiple Ways. Do You Talk About Your Entire Work History? Do You Bring Up Hobbies? What Should You Focus On? The Interviewer Isn't Interested In Your Personal Life. They Want To Know Whether You Can Handle The Job, What Accomplishments You Have Achieved, And How You Will Fit Into The Organization.

There Isn't A Wrong Way To Answer This Question, But There Is A Great Way To Answer The Question. Your Response To This Question Should Be Figured Out Before The Interview Even Begins. You Should Start Off By Reviewing And Fully Understanding The Job Description. Figure Out What The Hiring Manager Is Looking For And Understand What They Want Out Of The Ideal Candidate. Your Response Should Focus On Your Work Experience And Accomplishments, As It Relates To The Position You Are Interviewing For. Keep It Brief And Sell Yourself. Your Response Should Last About 30 To 45 Seconds.

For Example, After Introducing Yourself, Talk About Your Work Experience And Background As It Relates To This Position. Afterwards, Share Your Accomplishments, Such As Any Awards Or Recognition You Have Received. Anyone Can Talk About The Skills They Have For The Position, But Accomplishments Will Make You Seem Much More Credible.

What Are Your Strengths And Weaknesses?

Just Like The "Tell Me About Yourself" Question, Interviewers Usually Ask Candidates About Their Strengths And Weaknesses. They Want To Know How Your Strengths And Weaknesses Align With The Needs Of The Position. This Will Give The Interviewer An Idea Of How Suitable You Are For The Position.

Let's Start Off By Focusing On Your Strengths. If You Did Your Homework, You Will Know What Strengths Are Needed In The Position You Are Interviewing For. The Strengths You Share With The Interviewer Can Be Knowledge Based, Transferrable Skills, Or Personal Traits. More Important

Than The Strength You Share Is The Story Behind It. After You Tell The Interviewer About One Of Your Strengths, Share A Story That Illustrates That Strength In Action. If You Tell The Interviewer That Sales Is One Of Your Strengths, Share A Story About Any Awards You May Have Received From A Previous Employer, How You Ranked Amongst Your Peers, Or How You Were Asked To Facilitate A Sales Training Session For New Hires.

Now Let's Take A Look At How To Share Our Weaknesses. This Is Probably The Most Dreadful Part Of An Interview. Everyone Has Weaknesses, But Of Course No One Wants To Admit It. Why Would You? The Goal Is To Show How You Turned A Negative To A Positive. Select A Trait Then Explain What You Have Done To Overcome That Weakness. For Example, You Can Tell The Interviewer That You've Noticed That You've Had Trouble Handling Multiple Projects Simultaneously In The Past. In Order To Become More Organized, You Carry A Notepad Around With A List

Of Tasks You That Need To Complete Daily.

Conclusion

Everyone Must Earn A Living To Survive Unless You Were Lucky Enough To Be Born Into A Wealthy Family.

Even Then In This Case You Will Need To Fulfill Your Life By Pursuing A Career, Or Perhaps You Will Be Dedicated To Carrying On A Family Business.

Maybe You Are A Graduate Just Finished With Your Degree And Now Looking For Work In The Suitable Career Path. In Other Cases, You Were Miserable And Because Of This Quit Your Job To Look For Something Better. Lastly, You Could Have Lost Your Job Due To Downsizing Or Because The Company You Worked For Closed Its Doors.

Below Is A Summary Of Some Solid Tips Again.

Make Certain There Are No Mistakes On Your Resume Or Cv As It Is Called In Some Countries. Go Over It Carefully And Make Sure It Is In A Suitable Format Current With The Job Market Trends. Keep It

Short, Simple And Error Free While Ensuring You List All Your Skills And Relevant Information.

Make Sure You Are Well Prepared For An Interview By Following The Important Points We Have Listed In This Guide. This Preparation Gives You Confidence To Excel And This Will Help You Land A Good Job Or A Dream Job In Your Preferred Career Field.

Answer The Questions You Are Asked Without Rambling On And Stick To The Point When Answering. If You Do Not Have Proper Answers Then Do Not Be Afraid To Admit It. When Applying For Jobs Then Apply For The Ones That You Have Skills To Match. Sometimes This Is Not An Exact Requirement When The Company Is Offering Training.

If You Have Been Employed Before Then A Good Recommendation Or Referral From Your Previous Employer Can Go A Long Way To Helping You Get The New Job. As A Matter Of Fact, Referrals And Recommendations Increase The

Probability To Get The Job You Are Applying For Tenfold.

Recruitment Agencies Are Now Using The Convenience Of The Internet To Offer Positions Online, So Use This To Your Advantage For Applying Many Jobs Simultaneously.

www.ingramcontent.com/pod-product-compliance
Lightning Source LLC
Chambersburg PA
CBHW072007070526
44583CB00015B/1378